D1222671

BOURBON DESSERTS

Bourbon Desserts

LYNN MARIE HULSMAN

 UNIVERSITY PRESS OF KENTUCKY

Published by the University Press of Kentucky

Scholarly publisher for the Commonwealth,
serving Bellarmine University, Berea College, Centre
College of Kentucky, Eastern Kentucky University,
The Filson Historical Society, Georgetown College,
Kentucky Historical Society, Kentucky State University,
Morehead State University, Murray State University,
Northern Kentucky University, Transylvania University,
University of Kentucky, University of Louisville,
and Western Kentucky University.
All rights reserved.

Editorial and Sales Offices: The University Press of Kentucky
663 South Limestone Street, Lexington, Kentucky 40508-4008
www.kentuckypress.com

Library of Congress Cataloging-in-Publication Data
Hulsman, Lynn Marie.
  Bourbon desserts / Lynn Marie Hulsman.
    pages cm
  Includes index.
  ISBN 978-0-8131-4683-6 (hardcover : alk. paper) —
ISBN 978-0-8131-4685-0 (pdf) — ISBN 978-0-8131-4684-3 (epub)
1. Cooking (Whiskey) 2. Desserts. I. Title.
  TX726.H86 2014
  641.6'25—dc23
                    2014010374

This book is printed on acid-free paper meeting
the requirements of the American National Standard
for Permanence in Paper for Printed Library Materials.
♾

Manufactured in the United States of America.

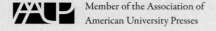 Member of the Association of
American University Presses

Dedicated to my brother Mark,

a proud Kentuckian who loved a glass

of good bourbon.

Contents

Introduction

Bourbon does for me what the piece of cake did for Proust. —WALKER PERCY

I come from a long line of bourbon lovers. As a Kentucky-born daughter of Kentucky-born parents, who themselves were born to Kentucky-born parents, it's my birthright to claim the warming, sumptuous elixir as my own when a bartender asks, "What's your drink?" True to my heritage, I'm flooded with fond memories with just one evocative whiff of the liquid gold that is bourbon.

I may live in New York City now, but please don't stir rye whisky into my Manhattan, like some beverage historians recommend. I take mine with Maker's Mark, thrilling each time a mixologist reaches for the sturdy, familiar, fat-bottomed bottle with the red wax dripping down its neck.

Breathing in the rich caramel aroma, laced with oak and a hint of rich vanilla pound cake, I'm transported back to my grandmother's house in the Germantown section of Louisville, cozied up next to her on the sofa, eight years old and freshly jammied, safe in the bend of her knees we called "The Bird's Nest."

"Herm, will you bring us a nightcap?" she'd ask my grandfather, eyes twinkling. Suddenly, an ordinary evening became a party, and I felt very grown-up indeed to be invited. Mine was always presented in a four-ounce juice glass, on a plate alongside whatever cookies happened to be in the jar. It was mostly ice cubes and Sprite, but there was no mistaking the fragrance and flavor of the scant teaspoon of bourbon that transformed my drink into a "highball," or the sociable feeling I got when we all clinked glasses in a convivial "Cheers!"

To me, bourbon signifies coming together with family and friends, slowing down to savor moments of sweetness and joy. Celebration. Connection. Reward.

And that's also how I feel about dessert.

Together, bourbon and luscious butter- and sugar-laced baked goods are natural partners, enjoyed in moderation as a pleasure for the senses. As with so many things in our lives, excess isn't the name of the game, but when we allow ourselves to truly experience the depth of quality spirits and homemade treats, a just-right amount infuses life with pleasure.

Even now, one sip of warming bourbon gives me a Christmassy feeling, the spicy heat teasing out memories of the fragrant liquor my mother added to her locally famous, creamy-centered, chocolate-covered bourbon balls the way one would pure vanilla extract. My mother was never a drinker, but she was an alchemist when it came to blending flavors, and bourbon was a natural partner to the sweet and bitter nuances of this holiday favorite. I'd like to think she concocted this annual treat as an homage to her father, who at age fifteen spent nights in jail as a stand-in for his own father, who ran a still in western Kentucky, near Franklin, as he scraped to support his family. Irish by descent, my great-great grandfather carried the family's proprietary liquor-making techniques from across the pond long before many other immigrants arrived at Ellis Island.

I'd wait by Mom's elbow while she beat the candy cream using down-home elbow grease, then help her hand-roll the confection into balls that would be enrobed in the melted dark chocolate that stood by. Perched atop a chair by the counter, I'd help her press buttery pecan halves onto the crown of each decadent piece as a finishing touch.

I was lucky enough to inherit the few mismatched commemorative Derby glasses that survived from the collections of my mother and grandmother. They take place of pride in the front of my china cabinet, reminding me of homespun, backyard, first-Saturday-in-May parties with the grill fired up and excitement for the big race sizzling through the air along with the mayflies. Derby Day, not Memorial Day, is the official day when Kentucky ladies don the first white shoes of the season, and the women in our circle marked the occasion with gusto, breaking out their sundresses or festive pastel T-shirts, emblazoned with Kentucky Derby logos.

Fizzing with excitement, friends and family would pile their paper plates high with barbecued chicken (drenched in a sweet bourbon, brown sugar, and vinegar sauce), German potato salad, and coleslaw, washing it all down with highballs and juleps made in these very glasses, printed with the names of the horses who claimed victory in every Run for the Roses since Aristides, in 1875. And of course, there were desserts, tangible evidence of the sweetness of the occasion: nutty Derby pie, salty-sweet chocolate-chip cookies, trifle bowls layered with Nilla Wafer banana pudding,

German chocolate cake, and ambrosia made with mini-marshmallows and jarred maraschino cherries. We traded dollar bills for slips of paper with the names of horses written on them, drawn out of a huge salad bowl, gambling on chances to win the pot. And we celebrated together, toasting with the signature drink of our state.

I'm proud that the popularity of bourbon has caught fire during this past decade, and that my beloved beverage is being enjoyed far beyond the borders of the Bluegrass State. Bourbon is not only being imbibed in cocktail bars and barbecue joints far from Bourbon County, Kentucky; it's being manufactured elsewhere, too. Although around 95 percent of production still occurs within Kentucky's borders, bourbon now springs forth from pioneering new distilleries in states such as California, New York, West Virginia, Wyoming, Illinois, Arkansas, and Florida. It gives me a warm feeling to know that bourbon's new-found wide appeal means that it's no longer simply a boutique beverage. Ready availability means that a new stripe of bourbon aficionados can feel like Kentuckians in their hearts, even if their feet have never tread on our state's soil.

That being said, I'll admit to enjoying a bourbon on the rocks just that small bit more if I'm in Louisville, perched on a stool at Timothy's on Broadway, or when it's served with a blue-cheese burger at The Bristol on Bardstown Road, or, especially, seated with old friends at a dark table at Jack Fry's. Bourbon caresses our senses, stirring dormant memories. I find the ones evoked by the aroma, warmth, and distinctive flavor of bourbon worth revisiting.

In 1983, the government of Kentucky officially declared milk as its state beverage, but I know the truth. Bourbon is Kentucky's true state drink. That truth calls me back to Derby Day after Derby Day to toast my Old Kentucky home with a freshly made mint julep and a slice of traditional Derby pie.

I Cakes, Sweet Breads, and Other Fluffy Delights

It seems there was never a time when I was growing up when the kitchen counter didn't feature some variety of baked good, ripe for the plucking. There was always my mom's renowned Jam Cake made with raspberry jam and caramel icing, or an apple cake stuffed to bursting with tender chunks of fruit, or the remnants of one of the myriad birthday cakes baked for one of the seven members of our family. What's more comforting than half of a pound cake waiting under the glass dome of a cake stand? I can't think of many things. Baked goods signal home and hearth. The care that goes into the preparation of such delights and their yielding softness when you ease a morsel into your mouth conspire to lovingly soothe and nourish those who partake.

The cakes, sweet breads, and other light and fluffy treats in this chapter are meant to envelop you in those very feelings, while at the same time awaken your sense of mischief and possibility by putting a bourbony twist on what you thought you knew by heart, and was done and dusted.

Pumpkin-Buttermilk Cake with Bourbon-Buttermilk Syrup

I've often wondered why baking with buttermilk ever fell out of favor. Perhaps this workhorse of an ingredient got left behind in the 1950s and '60s when American baking went the way of space-age laboratory science. I'm heartened to see a return to the old ways, and the days when housewives knew that adding buttermilk transformed cakes into fluffier, more tender pastries because it softened the gluten in flour. Plus, the trace globules of fat left behind when buttermilk is rendered enrich baked goods with both a creamy mouth feel and a distant hint of sourness.

I love this cake for its autumn-inspired pumpkin punch. Here, a basic pound cake is fortified with a can of pumpkin and a bouquet of warm fall spices. Not for the faint of heart, this spice cake relies on the bold flavors of ginger, clove, and cardamom, separating it from a basic pumpkin-pie flavored treat.

Glaze this moist cake with Bourbon-Buttermilk Syrup (page 4), and you'll elevate its status from basic workaday cake to liquor-kicked confection.

Makes one 12-cup Bundt cake (12 to 16 servings)

3 cups cake flour
2 teaspoons baking powder
1 teaspoon baking soda
1 teaspoon salt
1 teaspoon cinnamon
1½ teaspoons ground ginger
½ teaspoon ground nutmeg
½ teaspoon ground cloves
¼ teaspoon ground cardamom
1 cup (2 sticks) butter, at room temperature, plus more for greasing pan
1 cup granulated sugar
1 cup light brown sugar, packed
3 eggs
2 teaspoons pure vanilla extract
1 (15-ounce) can packed pumpkin
½ cup buttermilk
2 cups Bourbon-Buttermilk Syrup (page 4)

Preheat the oven to 350 degrees F. Liberally butter and flour a 12-cup Bundt pan.

Sift together the flour, baking powder, baking soda, salt, cinnamon, ginger, nutmeg, cloves, and cardamom into a medium mixing bowl and set aside.

Using an electric mixer, cream the butter, granulated sugar, and brown sugar on medium speed until fluffy, about 3 minutes.

Add the eggs, one at a time, beating to fully incorporate each before adding the next. Beat the mixture on medium-high for 5 minutes, until the mixture is fluffy and pale yellow in color.

Beat in the vanilla and pumpkin to combine. Then, at medium speed, add half the buttermilk, then half the flour mixture, combining the batter fully each time before adding the next ingredient. Repeat with the remaining buttermilk and flour.

Pour the batter into the prepared pan and bake 45 to 50 minutes, until a wooden cake tester or metal skewer inserted in the middle comes out clean. Cool the cake in the pan for 10 minutes, then gently turn the cake out onto a cooling rack; cool completely before cutting. (If you're topping with Bourbon-Buttermilk Syrup, pour one cup over the cake on its serving platter while the cake is still warm and let it soak in. Just before serving, pour the remaining syrup over the cake.)

Store in an airtight plastic cake safe or tin for up to 1 week.

❧ Bourbon Fact

You say potato, I say corn.

Keep your potatoes for your vodka, your grapes for your wine, and your juniper berries for your gin; the primary grain used in the distillation of bourbon is corn. In fact, the only spirits originating in the United States are corn-based: Tennessee whiskey and Kentucky bourbon.

Bourbon-Buttermilk Syrup

⟫ This syrup will win you over with its pale caramel color and bourbon-butterscotch taste. Equally at home on a stack of steaming flapjacks served with a cup of strong coffee and as a topping for steamed puddings and moist cakes, this bourbon-buttermilk syrup does journeyman's work. In my family, those with a sweet tooth have even been known to pour it over warm, buttered cornbread or "big as a cat's head" buttermilk biscuits.

The high proportion of fat from the butter in this simple concoction keeps the boiled buttermilk from separating, and that dab of baking soda mellows it down to smooth. Be sure to use a deep saucepan; the sauce will foam when you add the baking soda. The trick with this sauce is to stir constantly and to keep a sharp eye on it so it doesn't darken. As the syrup cools, the foam quiets down, and you'll be left with a lovely, honey-like color and consistency. My only warning is that you might be tempted to drink it directly from the serving jug; the two words that sum up this syrup are velvety and smooth.

Makes about 2 cups

½ cup (1 stick) butter
1½ cups light brown sugar, packed
1 cup buttermilk
2 tablespoons light molasses
¼ teaspoon salt
1 teaspoon baking soda
1 teaspoon vanilla
1 tablespoon bourbon

In a large, heavy-bottomed saucepan over medium heat, combine the butter and brown sugar. Stir until just melted, then add the buttermilk, molasses, salt, and soda. Using a whisk, stir briskly and constantly over medium heat; the mixture will foam up and then start to subside, but it will stay foamy and bubbly as you cook. Reduce the heat slightly and cook, still stirring constantly but more gently, about 5 minutes, until the syrup is a golden caramel color. Be careful not to let it get too brown. Remove from heat and stir in the vanilla and the bourbon.

Allow the syrup to cool completely in the pan, stirring now and then to reduce the foam and clear the syrup.

Store in a clean, tightly sealed bottle or jar in the refrigerator for up to 2 weeks.

Light Chocolate Layer Cake with Bourbon and Cream Cheese Frosting

For my money, the layer cake is the mother of all desserts. It's really two treats in one, and I can't decide which part is my favorite: the moist, satisfying cake or the creamy frosting that may as well be candy.

I especially love this cake as a vehicle for one of my favorite frostings. The cake is chocolate, to be sure, but with a subtler flavor than devil's food. Its delicate crumb and airy lightness make it a natural for stacking three layers high. With three layers, you get more frosting per bite. Given that I could eat Bourbon and Cream Cheese frosting spooned directly from the bowl, this construction only makes sense. Even so, I like to leave the sides of the cake bare; it reminds me of the kitchen-fresh creations raffled off at the cake wheels we'd bet on at Louisville's church picnics.

Makes three 9-inch rounds

1 cup unsweetened cocoa powder
   (I like Scharffen Berger's)
2 cups water, boiling
2¾ cups sifted all-purpose flour
2 teaspoons baking soda
½ teaspoon salt
½ teaspoon baking powder
1 cup (2 sticks) unsalted butter, at room temperature, plus more for greasing pans
2½ cups granulated sugar
4 large eggs, at room temperature
½ teaspoon pure vanilla extract

Preheat oven to 350 degrees F. Butter and flour three 9-inch cake pans.

In a medium mixing bowl, gradually add boiling water to cocoa while whisking until the mixture is smooth. Set aside and allow it to cool completely. (I like to do this step about an hour before making my cake. At the same time, I put the eggs and butter on the counter to bring them to room temperature.)

In a large mixing bowl, sift together the flour, baking soda, salt, and baking powder.

Using an electric mixer on high speed, cream together the butter and sugar until fluffy and pale yellow, about 5 minutes. Add the eggs, one at a time, mixing to combine after each, then add the vanilla. Beat until light and fluffy, about 5 minutes.

With the mixer on low speed, beat in the flour mixture and cocoa mixture, alternating about ¼ of each in turn. Beat only until combined; do not overbeat.

Divide the batter into the three prepared pans and bake for about 25 minutes, until a wooden cake tester or metal skewer inserted in the middle comes out clean. Cool the cakes in the pans set on cooling racks for about 15 minutes, then turn the cakes out onto the racks until completely cooled, about 30 minutes.

To frost the cake, place one cake layer on a platter; spread with about 1 cup of frosting. Top with another cake layer; spread with another 1 cup frosting. Top with the third cake layer; using a spatula, spread the remaining frosting in decorative swirls over the top of the cake, leaving the sides bare.

Once frosted, store in an airtight cake safe or tin in the refrigerator for up to 3 days.

ᐱ *Bourbon Fact*

Oui oui, y'all!

Bourbon is an American whiskey associated with Bourbon County, Kentucky. Current-day Bourbon County consists of a piece of what had been a larger tract of land that had been part of Virginia in 1785. Before that, the land was a section of French Louisiana, which explains the name *bourbon,* taken from the eponymous French royal family.

Bourbon and Cream Cheese Frosting

I'm the kind of girl who'll sip bourbon straight; I love the woody, multilayered flavor. I enjoy pairing bourbon with foods that offer a blank slate, so both the aroma and the flavor have the chance to pop. That said, when I find a taste that complements bourbon without stealing its thunder, I'm tickled. That's how I feel about the tang of cream cheese. Trust me: when you ease a forkful of this subtle, delicately flavored cake frosted with this special concoction, you'll wonder how your taste buds can delight to such different taste sensations without any one winning out over another. At this point, I've stopped wondering. I just close my eyes, sit back, and enjoy.

Makes about 3 cups

4 cups confectioners' sugar
2 (8-ounce) packages cream cheese,
    at room temperature
½ cup (1 stick) unsalted butter,
    at room temperature
1 teaspoon pure vanilla extract
2 tablespoons bourbon

Using an electric mixer set on medium-high speed, cream together the sugar, cream cheese, butter, vanilla, and bourbon in a medium bowl until smooth and creamy, about 5 minutes.

Store in the refrigerator, in a tightly lidded container, for up to 1 week.

Sinner's Chocolate Angel Food Cake

⟩ Growing up, I heard lots of talk from my Grandma and the ladies in her front-room, one-chair beauty salon about "reducing." Apart from cantaloupe and cottage cheese, or half a grapefruit with a maraschino cherry on top, the only virtuous dessert was angel food cake. I never cared for the sticky, Styrofoam-redolent packaged concoctions from the supermarket, though. Here's my twist: a homemade version that actually tastes like wholesome food. Perhaps it's a little lighter, with fewer calories than some desserts. I don't really care. I'm after thrills like bourbon and chocolate, and they're in there. Sinful? You decide.

Makes one 10 x 4-inch cake

1 tablespoon butter, for greasing pan
¾ cup all-purpose flour, sifted twice, plus more for flouring pan
½ cup cocoa powder (I like Scharffen Berger's)
1 teaspoon cream of tartar
½ teaspoon salt
1½ cups granulated sugar
1 cup egg whites (from 6 to 7 large or 8 to 9 small eggs), at room temperature
1 tablespoon bourbon

Grease a 10 x 4-inch tube pan with butter, dust it with flour, and set it aside.

Preheat the oven to 350 degrees F.

Sift the flour twice into a large mixing bowl, then measure it into another large mixing bowl. Add the cocoa to the flour, then sift together three times. Add the cream of tartar, and sift the dry mixture together one more time, then set it aside.

In a separate large mixing bowl, combine the salt and sugar, sift them together four times, then set aside.

Using an electric mixer set to medium-high speed, beat the egg whites until stiff but not dry, until you have medium-high peaks, about 5 minutes.

Sprinkle on enough of the flour-cocoa mixture to dust the top of the foam without collapsing it, then gently fold it in with a spatula. Alternate with small amounts of the salt-sugar mixture, and continue until all of the dry ingredients are folded into the egg whites.

Add the bourbon to the mixture, and fold in gently using the spatula.

Pour the batter into the prepared cake pan, and bake for 15 minutes at 350 degrees F. After 15 minutes, reduce the heat to 300 degrees F, and bake for 45 more minutes, or until a wooden cake tester or metal skewer inserted into the center of the cake comes out clean.

Invert the entire pan onto a wire rack on the countertop, and allow it to cool for two to three hours. Once it's cool, loosen the cake from the pan using a butter knife, and set it upright on a cake plate.

Store in an airtight plastic cake safe or tin for up to 1 week.

Kentucky Plus

- Use this as the base for a special strawberry shortcake.

- Make two, and layer chunks in a trifle bowl with vanilla pudding, Bourbon-Buttermilk Syrup (page 4), and fresh peach chunks.

- Dip chunks in chocolate fondue, and serve with mugs of coffee spiked with Orange-Bourbon Syrup (page 19).

Bourbon-and-Spice Glazed Peach Shortcake

Since moving north, I'm aware of a small empty place. An absence, if you will. I'm not entirely sure if it's in my heart or my brain. I ache with the distant memory of biting into a fragrant peach, so ripe that the delicate skin can barely contain the sweet, gushing juice inside. The kind of peach that drips down your chin and stains your blouse, but you don't care. You'd bite one again in a heartbeat, and you do. You can because when peaches are at their most perfect, they're cheap as dirt, so you have a bushel at your fingertips. Throw back a shot of bourbon with the nectar still on your lips, and you're transported to heaven. That just doesn't happen this side of the Mason-Dixon line.

Makes about 6 to 8 individual shortcakes

FOR THE SHORTCAKES
1¾ cups all-purpose flour
¼ cup granulated sugar, plus more for sprinkling
2 teaspoons baking powder
¼ teaspoon salt
½ cup (1 stick) unsalted butter, cold
½ cup heavy cream, cold
2 large eggs
2 teaspoons cold water
Confectioners' sugar, for garnish

FOR THE BOURBON-PEACH SAUCE
2 cups fresh peach chunks, from 5 or 6 large
    washed, pitted, and peeled peaches
½ cup sugar
¼ cup water
Juice of 1 small lemon
2 tablespoons bourbon
⅛ teaspoon ground ginger
¼ teaspoon ground cinnamon

FOR THE BOURBON WHIPPED CREAM
2 cups heavy cream, cold
2 tablespoons sugar
½ teaspoon pure vanilla extract
2 teaspoons bourbon

FOR THE PREPARED PEACHES
8 large fresh peaches, washed, pitted, peeled,
   and sliced into half-moons
½ cup granulated sugar

TO MAKE THE SHORTCAKES
Line a 9 x 13-inch baking sheet with parchment;
set aside.

Preheat the oven to 350 degrees F.

In a large mixing bowl, sift together the flour,
sugar, baking powder, and salt. Chop the cold
butter into small pieces. In a large mixing bowl,
combine the flour mixture and the butter, and
chill in the freezer for 15 minutes.

After 15 minutes, take the bowl from the freezer
and beat the ingredients together on low speed
using an electric mixer, about 3 minutes, until the
mixture looks like small, sandy marbles.

In a separate bowl, whisk together the heavy
cream and egg until combined, about 2 minutes.
Add the cream-egg mixture to the bowl containing the flour-butter mixture, and mix on low speed
using your electric mixer until dough forms, about
3 or 4 minutes.

Turn the dough out onto a lightly floured surface. Roll into a rectangle about half an inch thick.
As you work, lightly dust the dough with flour as
needed to keep the dough from sticking.

Fold the dough into thirds (like you're folding a
letter), then rotate the dough so a long edge of the
rectangle faces you. Repeat this rolling and folding
process three times, then roll out the dough to a
thickness of about ½ inch.

Using a 3-inch round cookie cutter (or a drinking glass with a floured rim), punch out rounds.
Place the cakes on the prepared baking sheet,
making sure to space them evenly. Roll the scraps
into a ball, and repeat the folding and punching
process until all the dough has been used. Chill
the rounds in the freezer on the baking sheet for
about 20 minutes.

While the cakes chill, use a fork to beat
together the egg and 2 teaspoons water in a small
bowl. Using a pastry brush, lightly coat the tops
of the cakes and sprinkle with sugar. Bake until
golden brown, about 20 to 25 minutes.

Remove the cakes from the oven and transfer
them to wire cooling racks.

TO MAKE THE PEACH SAUCE

In a medium saucepan, over medium heat, combine the peaches, sugar, water, lemon juice, bourbon, ginger, and cinnamon, and bring to a boil.

Reduce the heat and let simmer until the peaches cook down and a syrup forms.

Carefully pour the hot mixture into the carafe of a blender, and puree until smooth. Cover and refrigerate to chill, about 30 minutes.

TO MAKE THE WHIPPED CREAM

In a large mixing bowl (I use a metal one that I've chilled in the freezer), combine the heavy cream, sugar, vanilla, and bourbon, and beat with an electric mixer set to medium-high speed until soft peaks form, about 5 minutes. Cover and store in the refrigerator until ready to use.

TO PREPARE THE PEACHES

In a medium mixing bowl, toss the peaches with the sugar. Cover and allow to rest in the refrigerator for an hour, until a syrup forms.

TO ASSEMBLE AND SERVE

Mix the Bourbon-Peach Sauce into the bowl of Prepared Peaches, and set the mixture aside.

Using a fork, split the baked shortcakes in half horizontally. Lay the bottoms onto serving plate, cut side up. Top with a ladleful of the peach mixture, followed by a large dollop of the Bourbon Whipped Cream. Drizzle with a little more of the syrup from the peach mixture. Gently lay on the top of the shortcake, and sprinkle with confectioners' sugar for garnish.

Store any leftover shortcakes in an airtight plastic container for up to 3 days. Store any leftover peach mixture in a tightly covered bowl in the refrigerator for up to two weeks. Store any leftover whipped cream in the refrigerator, in a tightly lidded container, for up to 1 day.

Pineapple Upside-Down Cake with Bourbon and Salted Caramel

> Sweet and salty snacks drive us wild. Consider chocolate-covered pretzels, caramel corn, bacon bark, or the guilty pleasure of a hot, salted French fry dipped in a creamy vanilla milkshake. No matter what your flavor predilection, this cake will satisfy. Straddling fences to hit every mark, it offers tart fruit, warm spices, smoky bourbon, and sweet and salty caramel.

Makes one 9-inch cake

1 cup dark brown sugar, packed
1 cup (2 sticks) unsalted butter, at room
    temperature, plus 1 tablespoon for greasing
1½ teaspoons salt, divided
1½ cups all-purpose flour
2 teaspoons baking powder
½ teaspoon ground cinnamon
¼ teaspoon ground ginger
1 cup granulated sugar
2 teaspoons pure vanilla extract
3 tablespoons bourbon, divided
2 large eggs
¼ cup half-and-half
1 medium fresh pineapple, peeled, cored, and cut
    into rings, with 1 ring cut into chunks

Butter a 9-inch cake pan, and set it aside.

Preheat oven to 350 degrees F.

In a medium saucepan over medium heat, warm the brown sugar and ½ cup (1 stick) of the butter, whisking occasionally, until it becomes a smooth caramel sauce. Raise the heat to high and bring the mixture to a boil, whisking constantly; cook until it thickens and turns deep brown in color, about 4 minutes.

Remove the pan from heat and whisk in 2 tablespoons of the bourbon and 1 teaspoon of the salt. Pour the caramel sauce into the prepared cake pan, swirling to completely coat the bottom. Set aside and cool completely, about 20 minutes.

In a large mixing bowl, whisk together the flour, baking powder, remaining salt, cinnamon, and ginger.

In a separate large bowl, using an electric mixer set to medium-high speed, beat together the granulated sugar and remaining ½ cup (1 stick) butter until light and fluffy, about 3 minutes.

Add the vanilla and the remaining tablespoon of the bourbon, and beat to combine, about 1 minute.

Beat in the eggs, 1 at a time.

Reduce the mixer speed to low, and beat in the flour and spice mixture and ¼ cup half-and-half, about a third at a time.

Lay the pineapple rings over the caramel in the cake pan. Fill the spaces between the rings with pineapple chunks. Carefully pour batter over pineapple and smooth, using a rubber spatula dipped in warm water.

Bake for 45 to 50 minutes, or until a wooden cake tester or metal skewer inserted into the middle comes out clean.

Rest the pan on a wire rack to cool for about 45 minutes. Once cooled, run a butter knife around the sides of the pan to loosen the cake, then invert it onto a cake stand or plate.

Store in an airtight container in the refrigerator for up to 1 week.

❧ *How to Make Almond Flour*

If you ask me, almond flour is an excellent flour to have on hand for baking and pastry making. It adds a lovely, toothsome texture to many desserts; the nuttiness balances the sweetness of sugar; and if you have guests with certain dietary restrictions, almond flour can be used in kosher dishes and in gluten-free fare. Most recipes for almond flour call for blanched almonds, but feel free to experiment with whole almonds, as the skins add nutrition and flavor.

You can buy almond flour at many major supermarkets and at most health food markets. But if you're a do-it-yourself kind of person and you want to save a few pennies, making it yourself is a snap. (In cases where cross-contamination would inconvenience or endanger a guest, use dedicated equipment.) Place 1 cup slivered unblanched almonds in a clean electric coffee or spice grinder. Secure the lid, and pulse several times until you have a medium-fine textured flour. Be careful not to overgrind, or you will wind up with almond butter.

Transfer the flour to a clean flour sifter, and sift as you would wheat flour.

Remove any large chunks, and regrind.

Sift again. This should yield about 1 cup of almond flour.

Store in a tightly lidded container in the refrigerator for up to 2 weeks, or in the freezer for up to 3 months.

Iron Skillet Banana-Bourbon Upside-Down Cake

There's something romantic about cast-iron skillets. In this modern age of super-scientific Teflon and space-age, cheffy cookware, they hearken back to a time when cooking was done over an open hearth and in log-cabin kitchens. A cast-iron skillet is perfect for this banana cake. It distributes the heat for an even rise and moves easily from stovetop to oven. The cake itself is a celebration of sweet, caramelized banana mingled with bourbon toffee. Warm, light, and gooey, it's perfect with a hot cup of Joe (add a shot if you like!) or a tall glass of cold milk.

Makes one 12-inch cake

FOR THE CAKE
2 cups all-purpose flour
1¾ teaspoon baking powder
1 teaspoon ground cinnamon
¼ teaspoon ground cardamom
½ teaspoon salt
4 ounces (1 stick) unsalted butter,
   at room temperature
¾ cup granulated sugar
2 large eggs
1 teaspoon pure vanilla extract
2 teaspoons bourbon
¾ cup whole milk

FOR THE BANANA LAYER
4 tablespoons (½ stick) butter
½ cup dark brown sugar, packed
¼ teaspoon salt
3 tablespoons bourbon
3 to 4 small bananas, sliced lengthwise

Preheat the oven to 350 degrees F.

In a medium mixing bowl, combine the flour, baking powder, cinnamon, cardamom, and salt. Next, in a large mixing bowl, cream together the butter and sugar using an electric mixer set on medium-high speed until the mixture is light and fluffy, about 3 minutes. Add the eggs, vanilla, and bourbon and mix until smooth, about 2 minutes.

Add half of the flour mixture and half of the milk, and mix on medium-low until combined. Then, add the remaining flour mixture and milk, and mix for another minute or two, taking care not to overmix.

For the banana layer, melt the butter over medium heat in a 12-inch cast-iron skillet. Add the brown sugar and salt and stir with a heat-proof silicone spatula until the sugar begins to bubble, about 1 minute. Stirring constantly, carefully pour in the bourbon a little at a time (it will splatter and pop otherwise). Turn off the heat, and let the mixture cool in the pan for 10 minutes.

Next, arrange the bananas in the bottom of the pan, covering as much surface as possible. Pour the batter over the bananas, and smooth the top with a wet spatula.

Bake for 30 to 40 minutes or until the top is golden brown, the cake looks risen and crispy at the edges, and a wooden cake tester or metal skewer inserted into the middle comes out clean.

Remove from the oven and set the pan on a wire rack to cool for 20 minutes. Then, invert the cake onto a large serving plate and serve warm.

Store in a tightly lidded cake safe or tin for up to 5 days.

Kentucky Plus

- Substitute 8 canned apricot halves packed in syrup for the bananas.

- For a super-boozy treat, drizzle the cake with another shot of bourbon before serving.

- For a holiday spectacle, put the cake on a heat-proof plate, warm ½ cup bourbon on the stove, and ladle it over the cake. Use a long match to light the base of the cake. Once surrounded by blue flames, carry it to the table, set it down, and let flames die out.

Flourless Bitter Orange and Bourbon Cake

When I entertain, I want my guests to head home whispering, "I don't know how she does it." This super-simple cake, paired with equally simple but impressive Old Fashioned Cocktails, is one of my secrets. Light, moist, and a tad exotic, it's not as expected as your standard apple pie or chocolate cake. While simple, it is time-consuming, so I like to start making it on a lazy Sunday morning, taking long breaks to linger over coffee and the morning paper. By the time our early supper rolls around, I'm ready to wow the crowd. I'll share a lesson learned: Stick closely by the oven near the end of the bake time. As soon as the edges start to turn golden, take it out. Because of the oil from the almond meal, and the sugar, it goes from perfect to burned in the blink of an eye.

Makes one 9-inch cake

1 or 2 tablespoons butter, for greasing pan
2 medium, thin-skinned juice oranges (not navel), washed
3 large eggs
1 cup granulated sugar
2 tablespoons bourbon
1 teaspoon baking powder
3 cups almond flour (see "How to Make Almond Flour," page 14)
½ cup Orange-Bourbon Syrup with a Kick of Ginger (page 19)

Preheat oven to 350 degrees F. Butter a round 9-inch springform cake pan, and line it with parchment.

Place oranges in a medium saucepan and cover them with cold water.

Bring the oranges and water to a boil over medium heat, then reduce the heat and simmer for 15 minutes.

Drain the oranges and put them back into the saucepan, once again covering them with cold water. Repeat.

After 15 minutes, drain the oranges and refresh under cold water. Drain again, and move the oranges to a cutting board. Slice the oranges into thick rounds (about ¼ inch), then slice the rounds into half-moons. Remove the seeds, and discard.

Transfer the cooked orange slices to the carafe of a blender, or the bowl of a food processor. Pulse until you have a thin paste, the consistency of jam.

In a large mixing bowl, beat the eggs, sugar, and bourbon together using an electric beater until pale and thick, about 4 to 6 minutes. Beat in the baking powder to combine, about 1 minute.

Using a spatula, gently fold in the orange puree, then the almond meal, until just combined. Pour the batter into the prepared cake pan.

Bake for 1 hour or until a wooden cake tester or metal skewer inserted into the center comes out clean. Set the cake in its pan on a wire rack, and allow it to cool for an hour. After an hour, run a butter knife around the edges of the pan, and invert the cake onto the wire rack. Gently peel off the parchment, and set the cake right side up onto a cake stand or plate.

Use a skewer to prick 10 or 12 holes in the cake, then top with orange-bourbon syrup, Allow the cake to sit for at least an hour before serving. Store in the refrigerator, tightly covered with plastic wrap or foil, for up to 3 days.

Orange-Bourbon Syrup with a Kick of Ginger

There's no denying that a Bourbon and Ginger is a true Kentucky staple. I'd go so far to say that it should be the official highball of the state. Picture it garnished with an orange wheel. Distill the bright citrus flavor, the woodsy bourbon scent, and the warm spicy notes of ginger, and sweeten it with a bit of sugar. That's this syrup. I make double and triple batches and use it for refreshing sodas, to soak sponge and pound cakes, and to drizzle on dessert plates before laying on slabs of fruit pie.

Makes about ½ cup

2 large thin-skinned oranges (not navel), washed
¾ cup water
1 half-inch by half-inch piece of fresh ginger, washed, peeled, and cut into coin-sized discs
¾ cup granulated sugar
1 tablespoon bourbon

Using a vegetable peeler, remove the rind from the oranges, taking care not to press hard enough to sink deep into the bitter white pith. Cut the rind into thin strips, about ¼ inch wide and 2 inches long. Set it aside.

Using a small, sharp paring knife, peel away as much of the pith as you can from the oranges, and discard it.

Using a citrus reamer, juice the oranges, and discard the membranes.

Place the orange rind in a small saucepan with the water, and simmer it until soft, 7 minutes.

Drain the rind, then return it to the pan and add the ginger pieces, orange juice, sugar, and bourbon. Simmer the mixture over low heat, stirring occasionally, until the sugar dissolves and the syrup thickens, about 7 minutes.

Remove the syrup from the heat and pour it through a fine-mesh strainer. Discard the orange rind and ginger pieces, and allow the syrup to cool for 5 minutes, if you're using it to top a Flourless Bitter Orange and Bourbon Cake (page 17). If storing the syrup, allow it to cool for 20 minutes, then decant it into a clean, tightly lidded jar or bottle, and refrigerate for up to 2 weeks.

Light and Crispy, Just the Way We Like It

I can't recall ever hearing a southerner say, "Hell no, I don't want me no damn fried food!" At any rate, I can assure you I've never said it. That's because southern folk know how to fry things up right. Is there anything more sublime than a piece of chicken that's perfectly crispy on the outside and bursting with juice on the inside? Or a buttery, crusty hush puppy that's fluffed up and steamy in the middle? Or my favorite indulgence, cake-style doughnuts sprinkled with powdered sugar while they're still warm?

There's a learning curve to frying, and it's my theory that down south, practice has made perfect. Here are a few tips to help beginners avoid common pitfalls.

- Choose an oil with a high smoke point. There should be as big a difference as possible between the smoke point of the oil and the cooking temperature recommended. For basic frying at 375 degrees F, use canola, safflower, or grape-seed oil.
- Use a spatter screen to protect your skin and make cleanup a breeze.
- Use deep pans for frying. Leave a margin of at least 2 inches at the top of the pan to prevent spattering, and guard against overflow when adding food.

- When your oil is at the optimal frying temperature, sprinkle in a large pinch of kosher salt to reduce popping when food is introduced.
- Use a skimmer (also known as a spider) to add food to hot oil if you're nervous about getting your hands burned. It's a combination spoon and strainer, featuring an extra-long handle. If you don't have one, use a slotted ladle or spatula to lower food gently into hot oil; never drop it from high above. A skimmer is also the essential tool for lifting out cooked food.
- Keep all tools, such as skimmers and tongs, pointed down to prevent hot oil from rolling up the handles.
- Always work in small batches. Oil temperature lowers the second you add food.
- Monitor the oil temperature carefully and make sure it rises to at least what the recipe recommends or to slightly above it. When food particles flake into the frying oil, the smoke point lowers. A lower smoke point increases the chances of a grease fire.
- Use a deep-frying thermometer. Oil that's not hot enough yields soggy, greasy results. Oil that's too hot will result in burned outsides and raw centers. Your best bet is a thermometer with a large face that clips securely to the pot.

Drunken Hot-Fudge Pudding Cake

Deep, dark, and fragrant, the look and smell of this concoction promise to satisfy myriad cravings before it's even out of the oven. But most home bakers are sold on the idea before they pull out the first measuring cup. The mere mention of fudge, pudding, and cake are enough to drive someone wild. Add the word drunken, hinting at a boozy element, and even the most reserved among us begin smacking their lips.

The miraculous alchemy of this cake lies in the texture. No stone is left unturned. As it bakes, a rich, gooey cake appears on the top, and a velvety, melty sauce forms on the bottom. If you're lucky enough to get one of the edge slices, you'll be treated to a crispy crunch as an extra bonus.

Makes 9 servings

1 cup flour
2 teaspoons baking powder
½ cup cocoa, divided (I like Scharffen Berger's)
½ teaspoon salt
1 cup brown sugar, divided
½ cup milk
2 teaspoons vanilla extract
1 egg yolk
1 tablespoon bourbon
4 tablespoons (½ stick) butter, melted,
    plus 1 tablespoon, chilled, for greasing pan
½ cup semisweet chocolate chips
1 tablespoon instant espresso powder
½ cup hot water

Preheat oven to 350 degrees F. Butter a 9-inch square cake pan.

In a large bowl combine the flour, baking powder, ¼ cup cocoa, salt, and ½ cup brown sugar. Whisk to combine. Add the milk, vanilla, egg yolk, bourbon, and melted butter. Spread into the prepared pan.

In a small bowl combine the remaining brown sugar and cocoa. Whisk to combine and break up clumps.

Sprinkle the chocolate chips over the cake batter, distributing evenly, then sprinkle on the cocoa-sugar mixture.

Combine the espresso powder with the hot water and pour it gently over the top, but do not stir.

Bake for about 40 minutes or until the edges of the cake set up and brown, but the center still has a bit of jiggle. The middle part of the cake should look like a warm, rich custard.

Cool the entire pan on a wire rack for about 20 minutes before cutting into 9 squares. Serve warm.

Store in the refrigerator, tightly covered with plastic wrap or foil, for up to 1 week. Rewarm before serving.

Bourbon Fact

Don't call just any old whiskey bourbon. You might be in violation of the law!
To meet the legal definition of bourbon, a whiskey must be:

- Made from a grain mixture that is at least 51 percent corn.
- Aged in new charred-oak barrels.
- Distilled to no more than 160 proof, or 80 percent alcohol by volume. (In practice, most bourbon is distilled out at a lower proof than this.)
- Entered into the barrel for aging at a proof no higher than 125, or 62.5 percent alcohol by volume.
- Bottled at no less than 80 proof, or 40 percent alcohol by volume

Lemon-and-Bourbon-Cream Stuffed French Toast

❧ The perfect summer brunch dish, Lemon-and-Bourbon-Cream Stuffed French Toast is blushingly simple to prepare. To make a good thing even better, this delight stores well in the refrigerator before baking, so you can assemble it in advance. As a sweet main course for a festive breakfast, or an afternoon eye-opener served alongside a cup of hot tea with a slice of lemon, it's a treat that's toothsome enough to satisfy, with sunny-bright lightness that won't weigh you down.

Makes 9 servings

1 tablespoon butter, at room temperature, for greasing pan
8 large slices (about an inch thick) sourdough bread from a large pullman, or 12 to 16 slices if from a sliced loaf of sandwich bread, crusts removed, and cut into 1-inch cubes
1 (8-ounce) package cream cheese, cold, cubed
1 cup Bourbon Lemon Curd (page 174) or store-bought lemon curd
6 large eggs
1 cup milk
¼ cup granulated sugar
1 tablespoon bourbon
¼ teaspoon salt
3 or 4 tablespoons confectioners' sugar, for garnish

Butter an 8-inch square cake pan. (If making ahead, use a metal or tempered glass dish. Transferring a ceramic or earthenware dish from extreme cold to extreme heat will cause it to crack.)

Line the pan with half of the bread cubes. Distribute the cream cheese cubes evenly over the bread. Spoon dollops of lemon curd over the cream cheese, and cover with the remaining bread cubes.

In a medium mixing bowl, combine the eggs, milk, sugar, bourbon, and salt, and whisk together until combined. Pour the egg mixture over the bread.

Cover and refrigerate overnight, if making ahead. Or you can make it and bake it the same day.

If you've made it ahead, take the pan out of the refrigerator, uncover, and allow the pan to come to room temperature for 30 minutes. Whether you've made it in advance or on the same day, preheat oven to 350 degrees F, and bake the pudding for about 35 to 40 minutes.

Allow the entire pan to cool on a wire rack for about 15 minutes before dusting liberally with confectioners' sugar. Cut into 9 squares, and serve warm.

Store in the refrigerator, covered tightly with plastic wrap or foil, for up to 5 days.

Bourbon-Flapjack Coffee Cake

This cake offers up a farmer's breakfast all in one dish, if you're the kind of farmer who enjoys a little shot of Kentucky pick-me-up with his coffee. In the spirit of feeding hardworking folk, I've used almond flour so the treat eats like a meal; it stays with you and sticks to the ribs. Don't be tempted to use artificial maple syrup. The real deal makes all the difference in this recipe.

Makes one 9-inch cake

FOR THE CAKE

1 cup all-purpose flour, plus more for flouring pan
2 cups almond flour (see page 14)
2 teaspoons baking powder
½ teaspoon salt
½ cup (1 stick) unsalted butter, at room
    temperature, plus more for greasing pan
1 cup granulated sugar
3 large eggs, separated, at room temperature
2 teaspoons pure vanilla extract
2 teaspoons bourbon
½ cup whole milk

FOR THE SYRUP

½ cup sugar
¼ cup pure maple syrup
¼ cup coffee, cold
¼ cup bourbon

Preheat the oven to 350 degrees F. Butter and flour a 9-inch springform pan, then set it aside.

In a large mixing bowl, whisk together the all-purpose flour, almond flour, baking powder, and salt.

In a separate large bowl, combine the butter and sugar, and cream together using an electric mixer until light and fluffy, about 3 minutes. Add the egg yolks one a time, and beat for about 1 minute after each. Beat in the vanilla and bourbon until combined, about 2 minutes.

Add the dry ingredients mixture and the milk, a little at a time, alternating each. Beat well after each addition, about 30 seconds to 1 minute.

Wash and thoroughly dry the beaters.

In a large metal mixing bowl, beat the egg whites to glossy, almost-stiff peaks, about 5 minutes. Take care not to beat them till dry. Using a rubber spatula, gently fold the egg whites into the batter. Wash, but don't dry, the spatula.

Pour the batter into the prepared pan, and gently smooth the surface using the wet spatula.

Bake for 35 to 40 minutes, or until a skewer or toothpick inserted into the center comes out clean. Set the pan on a wire rack to cool.

Meanwhile, make the syrup.

In a small saucepan over medium heat, combine the sugar, maple syrup, coffee, and bourbon, and bring the mixture to a boil. Once it boils, reduce the heat to low, and simmer until it thickens to the consistency of warm honey, about 5 or 6 minutes.

Pour half of the syrup directly over the cake in the pan, distributing it evenly. Reserve the other half.

Let the cake stand for an hour or two before removing from pan. Cut into slices and serve with the remaining syrup.

Store in the refrigerator, with the cake and the sauce each in a tightly lidded plastic container, for up to 3 days.

Always-in-the-Pantry Bourbon Pound Cake

Deceptively simple, pound cake features very few ingredients, and the techniques involved are basic to baking. What this means is that every little detail counts. In order to get a light, moist, buttery cake, you have to be a little fussy.

The eggs need to be at room temperature, the butter should be of the highest quality, all-purpose flour steps aside in reverence to cake flour, and beaten eggs should be whisked full of air. Butter that's too warm or batter that's overbeaten will yield a flat, dense cake.

It goes without saying that if you're putting this kind of love and attention into a cake batter, you don't want to throw in cheap rotgut. Use top-shelf bourbon.

The loveliest thing about pound cake, though, is that it's rootsy; it's made from ingredients any farm wife has on hand. I recommend learning the basics of baking by making this cake again and again. I'm pretty sure your family won't complain.

Makes two 8 x 4-inch loaves

2 cups (4 sticks) butter, cold (but not hard),
   plus more for greasing pan
2½ cups granulated sugar
7 large eggs, at room temperature
4 cups cake flour, sifted before measuring
1 tablespoon bourbon

Butter the two pans and set them aside. Do not preheat the oven.

In a large mixing bowl, using an electric mixer set on medium speed, beat the butter 1 to 2 minutes, until it lightens in color. Add the sugar to the butter a little at a time, until it's all combined, then beat until light and fluffy, about 3 minutes.

In a separate small bowl, whisk the eggs until foamy, and set aside. With the mixer set on low speed, alternately add the eggs and flour, stopping to scrape the sides of the bowl occasionally. Add the bourbon and beat on low speed until just blended.

Divide the batter between the buttered pans, smoothing the tops with a spatula dipped in water. Put the pans, evenly spaced, in the cold oven, and set the temperature at 275 degrees F. After 30 minutes, increase the temperature to 350 degrees F and bake for 30 minutes; then rotate the pans. Bake for another 15 to 20 minutes, until a wooden cake tester or metal skewer inserted in the center of each cake comes out clean. If the tops are browning too quickly, cover loosely with a sheet of foil.

Cool the cakes on a wire rack in the pans for 30 minutes, then invert them onto the rack and cool for another hour before serving.

Store in an airtight plastic cake safe or tin for up to 1 week.

Smashed Sweet Potato Cheesecake

> ❧ This cheesecake is the perfect all-season dessert. Not too sweet and not too heavy, it's a great Easter Sunday dessert for its pretty, pale color and dairy-smooth creaminess. Because the sweet potatoes are canned, there's no need to chase down what's in season at the farmer's market.

Equally fitting on a Thanksgiving table, this cake reminds me of the buttery, hot yam casseroles that flanked my family's roast turkeys, always made with a touch of brown sugar and fall spice.

Makes one 9-inch cheesecake

FOR THE CRUST

¾ cup finely crushed gingersnap cookie crumbs
¼ cup finely chopped pecans
1½ tablespoons butter, melted, plus 1 tablespoon, chilled, for greasing pan
2 tablespoons granulated sugar

FOR THE FILLING

1 (15-ounce) can sweet potatoes in light syrup
2 (8-ounce) packages cream cheese, at room temperature
1 cup heavy cream
3 tablespoons all-purpose flour, plus more for flouring pan
2 tablespoons bourbon
1 teaspoon pure vanilla extract
½ teaspoon ground cinnamon
½ teaspoon ground nutmeg
¼ teaspoon salt
4 large eggs, separated

Preheat the oven to 325 degrees F. Butter and flour a 9-inch springform pan, and set aside.

In a large mixing bowl, combine the gingersnap crumbs, pecans, butter, and sugar, crumbling the mixture together with your fingertips. Then press it into the bottom and about ½ inch up the sides of the prepared pan.

Bake the crust for 5 minutes at 325 degrees. Remove from the oven and transfer the pan to a wire rack to cool.

Pour the entire can of sweet potatoes, including the syrup, into a large mixing bowl, and mash with a potato masher until smooth.

Add the cream cheese, cream, flour, bourbon, vanilla, cinnamon, nutmeg, salt, and egg yolks. Using an electric beater set to medium, beat until smooth.

In a separate bowl, using the electric beater set to medium-high, beat the egg whites until stiff, but not dry.

Using a rubber spatula, gently fold the egg whites into the sweet potato mixture.

Pour the batter into the prepared crust.

Bake on the center rack of the oven for 75 to 80 minutes.

Remove from the oven and cool on a wire rack, allowing the cheesecake to come to room temperature.

Refrigerate for about an hour, or until cold, before serving.

Store in the refrigerator, tightly covered with plastic wrap or foil, for up to 1 week.

Cinnamon Rolls with Bourbon Frosting

> Winter weekend guests smack their lips when they wake to find I've set to work early, making these cinnamon rolls and a pot of steaming hot, aromatic coffee. The spicy-sweet smell of the cinnamon mingled with the warm, smoky fragrance of bourbon fills the house and lures even the most reluctant to emerge from their cozy blankets.

What's special about this recipe is that the touch of potato transforms the dough, making it less glutinous and cloud light. The sleep you lose and the work you put in will pay off in spades with your appreciative friends and family.

Makes 1 dozen rolls

1 small Idaho baking potato, peeled and cut into ½-inch chunks
1½ teaspoons salt, divided
4½ cups all-purpose flour, plus more for sprinkling
1 cup granulated sugar, divided
2¼ teaspoons or ¼-ounce packet active dry yeast
¾ cup (1½ sticks) butter, at room temperature, divided, plus more for greasing pan
1 large egg
Canola oil, for greasing bowl
1 tablespoon ground cinnamon
2 cups confectioners' sugar
3 tablespoons whole milk
2 teaspoons bourbon

Grease a 9 x 13-inch glass baking dish with butter, and set it aside.

In a medium saucepan over high heat, cover the potato chunks with water (about an inch over the tops) and add ½ teaspoon of the salt. Cover the saucepan, bring the water to a boil, and cook the potato until it is fork tender, about 15 minutes.

Meanwhile, in a large mixing bowl, combine the flour, ½ cup of the granulated sugar, the yeast, and the remaining teaspoon of salt.

Drain the potato, reserving 1 ¼ cups of the starchy potato water, and put the potato chunks through a ricer. Add ¼ cup (½ stick) of the butter to the warm potato water and stir until fully melted. When the liquid cools, add it to the dry ingredients, along with the potato and the egg. Mix the batter with the dough hook attachment of a stand mixer set to medium speed or by hand until fully combined.

Knead the dough with the dough hook or turn it out onto a lightly floured surface and knead it by hand until it feels smooth and elastic, adding small amounts of flour to keep the dough from sticking.

Grease a large bowl with canola oil, put the dough ball inside, and turn it over a few times to lightly coat. Cover the bowl with a clean dish towel and let the dough rise for about an hour, or until it doubles in size.

Punch down the dough, then transfer it to a floured surface. Using a floured rolling pin, roll the dough into a rectangle, about 8 x 12 inches.

Spread the remaining ½ cup butter over the surface of the dough.

In a small bowl, combine the remaining ½ cup sugar with the cinnamon and distribute this mixture in a thin, even layer over the butter. Starting from one of the long sides, roll up the dough as tightly as you can. Cut the roll into 12 slices, and lay them in the buttered pan, cut side up.

Cover the pan with a clean dish towel and let the rolls rise for about an hour, or until they've doubled in size.

While the rolls rise, preheat the oven to 350 degrees F. When the rolls have finished rising, slide the pan into the oven and bake for about 45 minutes, until the rolls are golden brown on top. Meanwhile, in a large mixing bowl, whisk together the confectioners' sugar and milk, then whisk in the bourbon. Let the cinnamon rolls cool slightly, then drizzle on the icing and serve warm.

Store in an airtight plastic cake safe or tin for up to 3 days.

Bourbon Pecan-Pie Muffins

❧ Crisp on the outside and custardy smooth on the inside, these country cousins to pecan pie are an amazingly close taste match to the original thing. The bourbon flavor really stands out, adding a sophisticated twist. When you need to whip up a quick sweet to offer a surprise guest or to take to the bake sale that slipped your mind, these muffins fit the bill. If you have chocolate chips in the cupboard, throw in a handful to mimic Grandma Rose's Big Race Pie (page 76).

Makes 6 jumbo or 9 regular-sized muffins

Canola oil, for greasing muffin pan
1 cup light brown sugar, packed
¾ cup all-purpose flour
¼ teaspoon salt
¾ cup pecans, toasted and chopped
⅔ cup (1¼ sticks) butter, at room temperature
2 large eggs
¼ cup bourbon
1 teaspoon pure vanilla extract

Preheat the oven to 350 degrees F. Grease the muffin pan.

In a medium mixing bowl, using a fork, stir together the brown sugar, flour, salt, and toasted pecans.

In a separate bowl, using an electric mixer set to medium-high speed, cream the butter and eggs together until smooth, about 5 minutes. Add the bourbon and vanilla and beat for another minute to combine.

Next, stir the wet mixture into the dry mixture, using a fork, until just combined.

Spoon the batter into the prepared muffin pan, filling each cup about two-thirds full. Bake for 20 to 25 minutes, until muffins are golden brown on top and a wooden cake tester or metal skewer inserted into the center comes out clean.

Cool the pan on a wire rack for 15 minutes, then run a butter knife around the rims of the cups to loosen the muffins, and pop them out onto a serving plate.

Store in a cake safe or tin for up to 1 week.

Bourbon-Infused Orange Doughnuts

I love orange-flavored baked goods. They're such a refreshing change from more ubiquitous flavors like chocolate, vanilla, and cinnamon. And this recipe, with the zingy fresh ginger, is a breath of fresh air. These doughnuts are hearty enough for winter, and can stand up to a cup of bold coffee, but also work well in warmer months, with the eye-brightening citrus note. For a fluffy doughnut that's never greasy, make sure your oil is very hot (at least 365 degrees F). I like to make these in a very deep stockpot, with an extra-heavy, reinforced bottom. I'm not going to lie to you . . . frying these babies in lard brings a whole new nuance to decadent, but vegetable shortening or canola oil are fine alternatives.

Makes 1 to 2 dozen

1½ cups sugar, divided
2 tablespoons orange zest
1 cup orange juice
3 tablespoons bourbon
3 large eggs
4 cups all-purpose flour
4 teaspoons baking powder
½ teaspoon salt
2 teaspoons finely chopped fresh ginger
2 tablespoons butter, melted

In a medium mixing bowl, combine 1 cup of sugar, orange zest, orange juice, and bourbon, stirring lightly with a fork.

Using an electric mixer on medium speed, beat the eggs until light yellow, about 3 minutes. A little at a time, add sugar–orange zest mixture.

In a large mixing bowl, sift together the flour, baking powder, and salt.

Stir in the ginger.

Add the flour mixture to the egg mixture, a little at a time, beating until just combined, about 2 or 3 minutes for each of 2 or 3 additions. Do not overmix, or you'll have tough, flat doughnuts. Using a fork, stir in the butter.

Line two 9 x 13-inch baking sheets with parchment and sprinkle them liberally with flour. (Don't skimp!) Set one sheet aside.

Turn the dough onto the other sheet, and sprinkle flour over the top. Flatten the dough with your hands until it is about ¼ inch thick. If the dough is still wet, use more flour. Transfer the dough to the freezer until it's well chilled, about 20 minutes.

While the cut doughnuts chill, gather up the dough scraps, and repeat the flattening and cutting process.

Once the dough is chilled, take it out of the freezer. Using a doughnut cutter (or a 3- to 3½-inch drinking glass), cut out doughnut shapes. To cut out the holes, use your cutter (or an apple corer or the top of a small jar) to cut out circles of 1 inch in diameter.

Arrange the doughnuts and doughnut holes on the prepared sheet pan. Refrigerate the doughnuts for 30 minutes, or cover and refrigerate overnight to fry the next morning.

When you're ready to fry, put enough shortening into a deep-sided (but not wide) pan to measure a depth of about 3 inches. Clip a frying or candy thermometer to the side of the pan and heat over medium heat until the oil comes to 365 degrees F. Have several layers of brown paper ready for draining. (I use grocery bags.) Do not use paper towels, as the doughnuts will wind up limp and soggy.

Find the tools you'll need for flipping and lifting the doughnuts out of the oil, and lay them to the side of the stove. Once you start frying dough, things happen fast!

Pour the remaining ½ cup sugar into a large, wide bowl and set it aside.

Once your oil is ready, carefully add a few doughnuts to the hot oil, leaving plenty of space in between. Work in small batches so that the oil temperature doesn't decrease. Fry until one side is golden and crispy, about 1 minute. Turn the doughnuts over and fry until the other side is golden, about 30 to 45 seconds.

When the doughnuts are done, set them on brown paper to drain for a few minutes. While they are still warm, lay each doughnut on top of the sugar, then flip the doughnut and set the uncoated side on a serving plate. Serve warm.

Store in a tightly lidded plastic container or tin for up to 5 days.

Kentucky Mulled Cider and Bourbon Doughnuts with Cinnamon Sugar

I'll admit to being intimidated at the thought of making doughnuts until I witnessed my friend Chuck's salt-of-the-earth granny working magic in front of a pot of hot grease. Born in the days when people couldn't afford to buy baked goods, she could work any kind of dough and fry it up light and crisp, without ever glancing at a recipe. Her secrets were necessity and repetition. Even though you may not have years of experience under your belt, don't panic and run to the chain store. This easy dough is a great one to cut your teeth on, and the whole cooking process only takes about 20 minutes. But take my advice regarding the tools: invest in a frying thermometer and a doughnut cutter. They're cheap and easy to find, you'll only ever need one of each, and they don't take up much drawer space.

Makes about 14 to 18 doughnuts, plus the same number of doughnut holes (using a doughnut cutter roughly the size of mine, which is 2¾ x 1¼ inches)

FOR THE DOUGHNUTS
½ cup apple cider
½ cup applesauce
¼ cup bourbon
3½ cups all-purpose flour, plus more for dusting
    work surface
2 teaspoons baking powder
1 teaspoon baking soda
½ teaspoon ground cinnamon
½ teaspoon salt
⅛ teaspoon ground nutmeg
⅛ teaspoon ground cloves
¼ cup (½ stick) unsalted butter, at room
    temperature
1 cup granulated sugar
2 large eggs, at room temperature
½ cup buttermilk
Vegetable shortening (I use 1½ large tubs of
    Crisco)

FOR THE TOPPING
1 cup granulated sugar
1½ tablespoons cinnamon
½ teaspoon salt

TO MAKE THE DOUGHNUTS

In a medium saucepan over medium-low heat, simmer the apple cider, applesauce, and bourbon until it's reduced to about ¼ cup of syrupy liquid, about 25 minutes. Remove it from heat and allow to cool.

In a large mixing bowl, combine the flour, baking powder, baking soda, cinnamon, salt, nutmeg, and cloves. Set aside.

Combine the butter and sugar in a mixing bowl, and using an electric mixer set to medium-high speed, cream them together until light and fluffy, about 3 minutes. Add the eggs one at a time, beating after each, about 1 minute.

Reduce the mixer speed to low and gradually add the reduced apple-bourbon syrup and the buttermilk, alternating a bit of each, and mixing just until combined.

Add the flour mixture a quarter cup at a time, continuing mixing just enough for the dough to come together. Do not overmix or you'll have tough, flat doughnuts.

Line two 9 x 13-inch baking sheets with parchment and sprinkle them liberally with flour. (Don't skimp!) Set one sheet aside.

Turn the dough onto the other sheet and sprinkle flour over the top. Flatten the dough with your hands until it is about ¼ inch thick. If the dough is still wet, use more flour. Transfer the dough to the freezer until it's well chilled, about 20 minutes.

While the cut doughnuts chill, gather up the dough scraps and repeat the flattening and cutting process.

Once the dough is chilled, take it out of the freezer. Using a doughnut cutter (or a 3- to 3½-inch drinking glass), cut out doughnut shapes. To cut out the holes, use your cutter (or an apple corer or the top of a small jar) to cut out circles of 1 inch in diameter.

Arrange the doughnuts and doughnut holes on the prepared sheet pan. Refrigerate the doughnuts for 30 minutes, or cover and refrigerate overnight to fry the next morning.

When you're ready to fry, put enough shortening into a deep-sided (but not wide) pan to measure a depth of about 3 inches. Clip a frying or candy thermometer to the side of the pan and heat over medium heat until the oil comes to 350 degrees F. Have several layers of brown paper ready for draining. (I use grocery bags.) Do not use paper towels, as the doughnuts will wind up limp and soggy.

TO MAKE THE TOPPING

In a large mixing bowl, combine the sugar, cinnamon, and salt. Gently whisk together until fully combined.

TO FRY AND TOP THE DOUGHNUTS

Find the tools you'll need for flipping and lifting the doughnuts out of the oil, and lay them to the side of the stove. Once you start frying dough, things happen fast!

Once your oil is ready, carefully add a few doughnuts to the hot oil, leaving plenty of space in between. Work in small batches so that the oil temperature doesn't decrease. Fry until one side is golden and crispy, about 1 minute. Turn the doughnuts over and fry until the other side is golden, about 30 to 45 seconds.

When the doughnuts are done, set them on brown paper to drain for a few minutes. While they are still warm, lay each doughnut on the top of the cinnamon-sugar mix, then flip the doughnut and set the uncoated side on a serving plate. Serve warm.

Store in an airtight plastic cake safe or tin for up to 1 week.

Kentucky Plus

- For decadent bread pudding, use amounts of doughnut chunks equal to the bread.

- Top a doughnut with a scoop of vanilla ice cream and ladle on warm applesauce.

- Instead of coating with cinnamon-sugar, frost with Bourbon Cream Cheese Frosting (page 7).

Bourbony Butter Kuchen

The butter kuchen I grew up with came from a very old German bakery called Heitzman's in the Schnitzelberg section of Louisville, Kentucky's Germantown. The older folks I've spoken to seem to agree that this pastry, with its signature decadent, runny, chess pie–like filling, was a staple in most of the German bakeries dating back to shortly before the turn of the last century. My grandmother often laughed when she told me her guilty tale of making sure her family made off with a butter kuchen or two before they sold out on Sunday mornings in the 1940s and '50s. Either she or one of her brothers or sisters would skulk toward the back of St. Elizabeth's church, next door to the bakery, before the mass officially ended. There was always a Kamber sibling trailing the recessional of the priest and the altar boys, headed to the front of the line at Heitzman's.

Makes one 9-inch pastry

FOR THE DOUGH
⅓ cup warm whole milk
2¼ teaspoons (one ¼-ounce envelope) active dry yeast
2½ tablespoons sugar
2 tablespoons unsalted butter, melted, plus more for buttering bowl
1 large egg
½ teaspoon salt
1¼ cups all-purpose flour

FOR THE FILLING
½ cup (1 stick) unsalted butter, melted but not hot, plus extra for buttering
¾ cup granulated sugar
1 large egg
1 tablespoon water
1 teaspoon pure vanilla extract
1 teaspoon lemon juice
2 tablespoons bourbon
⅛ teaspoon salt
4 teaspoons all-purpose flour

TO MAKE THE DOUGH

Preheat the oven to 350 degrees F. Butter a large mixing bowl, and a 9-inch cake pan, and set them aside.

In a Pyrex measuring cup, warm the milk in the microwave on high for 30 seconds. Pour in the yeast and set it aside until the mixture is foamy, about 5 minutes. Transfer it to a medium mixing bowl, and gently stir in the sugar, butter, egg, and salt.

Using a fork, stir in the flour until a soft, wet dough forms. Place the dough in the buttered bowl, and cover it with plastic wrap.

Allow the dough to rise on the countertop until it doubles in size, about 1 hour. Punch down the dough and press it into the bottom of the buttered pan, with the edges slightly higher than the center. Cover the pan with a clean dish towel, and allow the crust to rise until puffy, about 45 minutes to an hour.

TO MAKE THE FILLING

In a large mixing bowl, whisk together the butter, sugar, egg, water, vanilla, lemon juice, bourbon and salt. Once combined, add the flour a teaspoon at a time, whisking between each addition until smooth, about 45 seconds.

TO ASSEMBLE

Press down center of risen dough, then gently and evenly pour in the filling.

Bake until golden brown at the edges, and the center is nearly set. It will look wobbly, like a custard, but will continue to set as it cools, about 30 minutes.

Transfer the pan to cool on a wire rack for 30 minutes. Serve slightly warm or at room temperature straight from the pan.

Store loosely covered in the refrigerator, for up to 1 week.

Lane Cake

⟫ Some food historians say this cake originated in Alabama, and still others trace its roots back to England. In the days when fresh fruit wasn't available in the winter, and sugar was considered more of a luxury than a staple, cake made with dried fruit was a Christmas extravagance. The custom of serving fruitcake during holiday celebrations, however, survived long after food preservation, mass production, and shipping methods became modernized. It's said that Lane Cake, a light white cake that utilizes fruit and nuts differently than fruitcake, was created to please those who didn't care for the denser, richer dessert. Regardless of how this sweet came into being, it now enjoys status as a traditional southern holiday classic. Generally speaking, the amount of cake batter needed for three 9-inch layer cake pans will also make around 24 cupcakes in standard muffin tins. This recipe can be made as a layer cake, using the three layer cake pans, or do what I like to do: use large ramekins that yield what most commercial bakeries call jumbo muffins.

FOR THE CAKE

3 cups cake flour, sifted before measuring, plus extra for flouring pans
2 teaspoons baking powder
¼ teaspoon salt
⅔ cup (11 tablespoons) unsalted butter, softened, plus more for buttering pans
2 cups granulated sugar
1 teaspoon pure vanilla extract
7 large egg whites, at room temperature
½ cup whole milk

FOR THE FILLING

½ cup butter
7 large egg yolks
1 cup granulated sugar
1 cup bourbon
½ teaspoon pure vanilla extract
½ cup raisins
½ cup dried cherries
1 cup coarsely chopped pecans
1 cup sweetened shredded coconut flakes

TO MAKE THE CAKE

Preheat the oven to 350 degrees F. Butter and flour the bottoms and sides of three 9-inch cake pans, or two 12-hole muffin tins, or 8 to 12 large ramekins. In a medium mixing bowl, sift together the already sifted flour with the baking powder and salt, and set it aside.

In a large bowl, using an electric mixer, beat the butter at medium-high speed until light and creamy, about 3 minutes. Gradually add the sugar, beating until fluffy, occasionally scraping down the sides of the bowl. Reduce speed to low, and add the vanilla, then beat just to combine, about 1 minute.

Divide the flour mixture into thirds, and alternate adding each part and a third of the milk to the butter-sugar mixture, beating briefly between each addition, about 30 seconds.

Transfer batter to large bowl; wash and completely dry mixing bowl and beater attachments. In the clean bowl of the electric mixer, beat the egg whites until they form soft peaks, about 3 to 5 minutes. Gently fold the beaten egg whites into the batter in thirds.

Pour the batter into prepared pans, and tap them on the counter to remove any air pockets.

Bake for 20 to 25 minutes, depending on whether you're using pans, tins, or ramekins. You'll know the cakes or muffins are done when you smell the aroma, the tops are lightly browned, and the cake springs back in the center when lightly pressed. Cool in the pans on racks for 5 minutes before inverting the cakes onto racks to cool completely.

TO MAKE THE FILLING

In a large saucepan, set over medium-low heat, melt the butter, then set it aside to cool.

In a medium bowl, beat the egg yolks using a whisk until light. Gradually whisk in the sugar until well blended. Now, beat in the bourbon and vanilla until combined, about 1 minute. Finally, beat in the melted butter until combined, about 1 minute.

Transfer the mixture to a medium saucepan, set over medium heat, and cook, taking care not to simmer, stirring constantly with a wooden spoon until the mixture is very thick and coats the back of the spoon, about 15 to 20 minutes.

Remove the mixture from the heat and stir in the raisins, cherries, pecans, and coconut. Refrigerate for 3 hours, or until fully cooled and thickened.

TO ASSEMBLE

If making a cake, invert 1 layer onto a large cake plate. Top with about 1 cup of the filling, and spread it to the edges in an even layer. Top with the second cake layer and spread that layer with another cup of the filling, again spreading it to the edges in an even layer. Repeat with final cake layer and remaining filling.

If making muffins, slice each muffin into three equal-sized layers. (You can mark where the cuts will take place with toothpicks, then "cut" the cake by pulling a fine thread through it for an even cut.) Spoon on a heaping tablespoon of filling, and repeat as you would for the cake.

Store at room temperature, in a cake safe or tightly lidded container, for up to 1 week.

2   Cookies and Bars

❧ Who among us doesn't remember bursting into the house as a child, starving after a long day of school? I know the first place I headed, and I'll bet anything it was the same for you: the cookie jar. It was so satisfying to grab a handful of chocolate chip or oatmeal raisin beauties and wash them down with a tall glass of milk. I'd worked hard. I deserved it.

As much fun as the eating was the baking. I started on buttering duty, making sure the baking sheets were evenly glossed. Stirring in the chips or nuts and eventually rolling out dough, or dropping batter onto a cookie sheet, filled me with pride. I was doing meaningful work, grown-up's work.

If we missed the main event, the youngest of my brothers and I might hear the muted whir of the electric mixer and sprint into the kitchen to investigate. We'd lick the beaters and fight over the bowl. Knowing hot cookies couldn't be far behind, we'd park at the kitchen table, basking in the warmth and fragrance. We were told to wait till they cooled, but Mom was a softie. She'd always cave and let us pick one out of the first batch, too hot to handle.

With the recipes in this chapter, I hope you'll enjoy the adult version of these childhood joys. Burst in from work, grab a few liquor-kissed cookies, and pour yourself a tall, cold highball. You work hard. You deserve it.

Browned Butter and Bourbon Biscuits

⬦ I understand that browning butter seems like an extra step, adding more labor to a simple cookie recipe. You have to trust me on this: it's worth it. The nutty depth of browned butter adds a flavor note not found elsewhere, and it is bourbon's soul mate. I'll admit that it's easy to burn the butter, but you shouldn't worry. A burned batch can be saved to sauce meats and vegetables, and starting over is as easy as pie.

Makes about 3 dozen cookies

¾ cup (1½ sticks) unsalted butter, cold
2½ cups flour
1½ teaspoons baking soda
½ teaspoon salt
¼ teaspoon ground cinnamon
¼ teaspoon ground nutmeg
⅛ teaspoon ground clove
1 cup light brown sugar, packed
½ cup granulated sugar
1 large egg, whole, plus 1 large egg yolk
1 teaspoon pure vanilla extract
3 tablespoons bourbon

To brown the butter for this recipe, chop it into small cubes and melt in a small, heavy-bottomed saucepan set over medium heat.

Stirring constantly with a wire whisk, cook the butter until it foams. As the foaming subsides, light brown specks will begin to form in the bottom of the pan. You'll know it's done when it turns amber and gives off a rich, nutty fragrance. When this happens, remove the pan from the heat, and keep whisking until the foam disappears. It only takes a minute to go from browned butter, to burned butter. If the butter blackens, you'll need to set it aside and start over for this recipe.

Don't waste the burned batch, though! Use it as *beurre noir* in a savory dish. Mix in some chopped sage leaves or garlic, cover it tightly, and store it in the fridge, and use it to top asparagus, Brussels sprouts, or cooked steaks just before serving.

Once you have the beautifully browned butter for this recipe, set it aside.

Preheat the oven to 325 degrees F. Line two 9 x 13-inch baking sheets with parchment and set them aside.

In a medium-sized mixing bowl, gently whisk the flour, baking soda, salt, cinnamon, nutmeg, and cloves together until blended. Set aside.

In the bowl of a stand mixer, combine the light brown sugar, granulated sugar, and the cooled browned butter. Using a paddle attachment with the mixer set on medium-high speed, mix until well blended. At this stage, the mixture will not look creamy like regular cookie batter, so be patient.

Add the egg, egg yolk, vanilla, and bourbon and, with the mixer set on low speed, mix until combined.

Add the flour mixture a little at a time, and mix just until blended, taking care not to overwork the batter.

Using a 2-ounce ice cream scoop, scoop the dough onto the prepared baking sheets. Bake in the preheated oven for 11 to 13 minutes, or until the cookies are crispy on the edges, but not too brown in the middle.

Remove from the oven and set the baking sheets on wire racks to cool for 5 minutes, then transfer the cookies directly onto the racks to cool for another 10 minutes.

Store in a tightly lidded plastic container or tin for up to 1 week.

Kentucky Plus

- Use these instead of ladyfingers to make a southern-style tiramisu.

- Crumble and layer these in parfait glasses with Burnt Sugar and Bourbon Pudding (page 95).

- Make grown-up ice cream sandwiches by stuffing these with Make Mine a Manhattan Ice Cream (page 128) and freezing until set.

Bourbon-Toffee Shortbread Biscuits

> Shortbread is to cookies what pound cake is to cake: the essence of the type. I love shortbread for its homey goodness. Basic and wholesome, you're likely to have the ingredients to make a batch in your pantry at any given time. You can treat shortbread like a blank slate and introduce flavors and textures without robbing it of its identity. The addition of bourbon and toffee to this basic dough is the icing on the cake, so to speak. Check the baking section of your supermarket for toffee bits sold in bags, like chocolate chips. If you can't find them, throw a couple of Heath or Skor bars in the freezer for an hour, break them up with a meat tenderizer, and use the pieces as a substitution.

Makes about 2 dozen cookies

1 cup (2 sticks) unsalted butter, at room temperature
½ cup granulated sugar
½ cup light brown sugar, packed
1 large egg yolk
2 cups all-purpose flour
½ teaspoon salt
½ teaspoon baking soda
1½ tablespoons bourbon
½ cup chopped almonds
½ cup toffee bits

Preheat the oven to 275 degrees F. Line two 9 x 13-inch baking sheets with parchment, and set them aside.

In a medium-sized mixing bowl, using an electric mixer at medium speed, beat the butter until creamy and light, about 5 minutes. Gradually add the granulated sugar, brown sugar, and egg yolk, beating until combined, about 1 to 2 minutes.

In a separate large mixing bowl, combine the flour, salt, and baking soda, mixing with a fork until combined.

Working a little at a time, add the flour mixture to the butter mixture, beating on low speed until blended.

Beat in the bourbon, almonds, and toffee bits until just blended, about 30 to 45 seconds. Cover and chill the dough for 20 minutes.

Turn the chilled dough out onto a lightly floured surface and roll it out to about a ½-inch thickness. Cut out rounds with a 2- to 2½-inch cookie cutter or with a drinking glass with a floured rim. Arrange the cookies about 2 inches apart on ungreased baking sheets.

Bake at 275 degrees F for 45 to 50 minutes. Remove from the oven and set the baking sheets on wire racks to cool for about 5 minutes; then transfer the cookies directly onto the racks, and cool for another 20 minutes.

Store in a tightly lidded plastic container or tin for up to 1 week.

Peanut Butter–Chocolate Chip Cookies with Bourbon and Bacon

⋗ "I know it's too much, but is it enough?" the old saying goes. My Aunt Donna brings this sentiment to life with her style. Dressing in a red top to liven things up isn't enough; she adds pedal-pushers with a repeating whole cherry print. Her Halloween parties are a legendary mash-up of homemade crafts, themed food, and costumes that get more outrageous by the year. When she hosts a holiday meal, don't expect meat, a starch, and two vegetables; it's like walking into the old Blue Boar cafeteria, where there were so many steam-table offerings you had to do strategic planning before picking up a plate. I love her for it, and I suspect I'm not alone. These cookies are like Aunt Donna. Your head might spin from the sheer number of tasty offerings, but would you really want to tone it down?

Makes about 2 dozen cookies

1¼ cups all-purpose flour
¼ teaspoon baking soda
¼ teaspoon baking powder
¼ teaspoon salt
6 strips bacon
4 tablespoons (½ stick) butter, at room temperature
½ cup natural peanut butter (do not used whipped and sweetened!)
½ cup granulated sugar
½ cup dark brown sugar, packed
1 large egg
2 tablespoons bourbon
⅓ cup bittersweet chocolate chips

Preheat the oven to 350 degrees F. Line two 9 x 13-inch baking sheets with parchment.

In a large mixing bowl, combine the flour, baking soda, baking powder, and salt. Mix together with a fork until well blended.

In a large, heavy-bottomed pan over medium-high heat, cook the bacon until crisp, about 3 to 4 minutes each side. Transfer the bacon to a few layers of brown paper bags to cool and drain (do not use paper towels or the bacon will go limp and soggy). Reserve 2 tablespoons of the bacon grease, and set it aside.

Once the bacon has cooled, crumble it into small bits, and set it aside.

In a large bowl, using an electric mixer set on medium speed, beat together the butter and bacon grease until smooth, about 1 minute. Beat in the peanut butter until well blended, about 1 minute. Beat in the granulated sugar and brown sugar until creamy, about 3 minutes, then add the egg and bourbon and beat until light and fluffy, about 2 more minutes.

A little at a time, add the flour mixture, and beat until just combined, about 1 or 2 minutes.

Using a wet, rubber spatula, stir in bacon and chocolate chips.

Using your wet hands, roll the dough into 1-inch balls and arrange about 2 inches apart on the baking sheets. Bake for 8 to 10 minutes, or until the edges crisp and the tops look golden brown.

Remove from the oven and set the baking sheets on wire racks to cool for about 5 minutes, then transfer cookies directly onto the racks to cool for about 10 more minutes.

Store in the refrigerator, in a tightly lidded plastic container or tin, for up to 1 week.

❧ *Bourbon Fact*

The bourbon barrel: A gift that keeps on giving.

Kentucky bourbon distillers ship gently used bourbon barrels to Scotland and Ireland for use in the maturation of Scotch and Irish whiskey.

Bourbon-Lemon Bars

➤ Lemon adds freshness to any dish. It offers its own bright flavor and sharpens the flavors it complements. In these smooth, rich bar cookies, the lemon serves to heighten the flavors of butter, salt, and, of course, bourbon. One thing to note: it's important that the filling be poured into a warm crust. Make the filling first, and set it aside. Right before pouring it in, give it a quick stir to blend, and you're good to go.

Makes 12 bars

FOR THE FILLING
6 large eggs, at room temperature
3 cups granulated sugar
2 tablespoons grated lemon zest (from 3 to 5 large lemons)
¾ cup lemon juice
¼ cup bourbon
1 cup flour
Confectioners' sugar, for garnish
1 sprig fresh mint, washed and cut into pieces, for garnish

FOR THE CRUST
1¾ cups all-purpose flour
⅔ cup confectioners' sugar, plus extra for garnish
¼ cup cornstarch
¾ teaspoon salt
¾ cup (1½ sticks) butter, chilled and cut into 1-inch pieces, plus more for greasing pan

TO MAKE THE FILLING
In a large mixing bowl, whisk together the eggs, sugar, lemon zest, lemon juice, bourbon, and flour. Chill filling in the refrigerator until the crust is ready.

TO MAKE THE CRUST
Adjust oven rack to middle position and heat oven to 350 degrees F. Lightly butter a 9 x 13-inch baking dish and line with one sheet of parchment or wax paper. Dot paper with butter, then lay a second sheet crosswise over it.

In the bowl of a food processor fitted with a steel blade, pulse the flour, confectioners' sugar, cornstarch, and salt together. Add butter and process to blend, about 10 seconds, then pulse until mixture is pale yellow in color and looks like small, sandy marbles, about three or four 1-second bursts.

Tip the dough onto a floured surface, and form it into a ball. Transfer the dough into the prepared pan.

Using your floured fingers, press the mixture into an even, ¼-inch layer over the bottom, and about ½ inch up sides. Bake the crust until golden brown, about 20 minutes.

Remove from oven and set the pan on a wire rack to cool for 10 minutes.

TO ASSEMBLE

Take the chilled filling from the refrigerator, and stir it with a fork to reblend. Pour the filling onto the crust, and bake for 25 to 30 minutes, until the middle is set.

Remove from the oven, set the pan on a wire rack, and allow it to cool for 30 minutes. Dust with confectioners' sugar, and cut into squares. Top each bar with a sprig of fresh mint, and serve.

Store in the refrigerator, tightly wrapped in plastic wrap or foil, for up to 5 days.

Thumbprint Cookies

 Thumbprint cookies garner oohs and aahs but are surprisingly easy to make. Everyone loves a bite of buttery cookie with the bonus of a dollop of a smooth, sweet treat. Like a filled doughnut or a jelly roll, it's all about the filling. More often than not, you'll be using jams, preserves, or curds you've already made (or bought) to fill the cookies, so half the work will already be done. If you like yours with the kick of bourbon, like I do, try these tasty shells filled with Boozetella (page 167), Bourbon Lemon Curd (page 174), or Bourbon-Cherry Jam (page 169).

Makes about 3 dozen cookies

1½ cups (3 sticks) butter, at room temperature
1 cup granulated sugar
1 large egg, at room temperature
3¼ cups all-purpose flour
¾ cup jam

Preheat oven to 350 degrees F. Line three 9 x 13-inch baking sheets with parchment.

In a large mixing bowl, using an electric mixer set on medium-high speed, cream the butter and sugar together until it's light and fluffy, about 3 minutes.

Add the egg, and beat until combined, about 1 minute.

Add the flour and mix just until incorporated and a stiff dough is formed, about 1 or 2 minutes.

Roll the dough into 1-inch balls. Arrange on baking sheets, at least 3 inches apart.

Moisten your thumb with water, and press it into the top of each ball, making a shallow pit about ½ inch wide and 1 inch deep.

Bake until cookies are golden brown at the edges, 16 to 18 minutes. Transfer the baking sheets containing the cookies to a wire rack and let cool for 15 minutes. Leave the oven on.

Once the cookies have cooled, heat jam until slightly runny; dollop about ½ teaspoon into each indentation. (If using Bourbon Lemon Curd, don't heat it; just dollop it in chilled.) Return the trays to the oven and bake for 1 to 3 minutes, or until curd or jam is set. (If using Boozetella, do not return the cookies to the oven.)

Store at room temperature, in a tightly lidded container, up to 3 days.

Nutty Bourbon Scotchie Bars

The bourbon whiff in these cookies is subtle. It's like an echo or a memory. That suits me fine, because the dough for these cookies is such a solid, homey staple, that it's pleasing enough on its own. The whisper of bourbon, though, renders it just that much more "Kentucky" to me. Even if Kentucky is not your homeland, I suspect you'll find the bourbon note in this recipe to be warm and enveloping, like the place you call home. The additional richness of the butterscotch calls to my mind centuries of mothers and grandmothers . . . butter, brown sugar, cream, and vanilla. All of them reliable and familiar ingredients, and all of them sublime. Feed these cookies to the blue and the homesick, and watch them relax into the layers of flavor, and come out the other side revived. Or keep things simple and just enjoy the simplicity of the sweetness and texture during a quiet moment all to yourself.

Makes 16 bars

¾ cup pecan halves
½ cup (1 stick) cup butter, plus more for greasing pan
1 cup light brown sugar, packed
1 cup dark brown sugar, packed
2 tablespoons bourbon
2 large eggs
1½ teaspoons salt
1 teaspoon baking powder
1½ cups all-purpose flour
1¼ cups butterscotch chips

Preheat oven to 350 degrees F. Butter a 9 x 13-inch pan.

Once the oven is hot, line a baking sheet or the tray of your toaster oven with foil, and spread the pecan halves in a single layer. Toast the nuts until golden brown, keeping a close eye on them. I've burned more than one batch by getting distracted. (Here's a hint: If you smell them, they're done.) Remove from the oven, set the baking sheet on a wire rack, and cool for 10 minutes. Chop the nuts coarsely, and set them aside.

Melt the stick of butter in the microwave. (I use a Pyrex measuring cup, covered with a paper towel.)

Pour the melted butter into a large mixing bowl and, using a fork, stir in the dark and light brown sugars and the bourbon; then set the mixture aside and let it come to room temperature, about 20 minutes.

Add the eggs, salt, baking powder, and flour, and mix until well blended. Stir in the butterscotch chips and pecan pieces.

Pour the batter onto the prepared baking sheet, and bake for 18 to 22 minutes, or until bars begin to pull away from the sides of the pan and the top is golden brown and shiny.

Remove from the oven, set the pan on a wire rack, and allow it to cool for 20 minutes. Once cooled, cut the bars into rectangles, and serve.

Store in the refrigerator, in an airtight, lidded plastic container or tin, for up to 1 week.

Hermit Cookies with Bourbon Glaze

What's not to like about hermit cookies? With a soft, chewy texture and the flavor of warming autumn spices, they're jam-packed with fruit and nuts. Legend has it that hermits got their moniker because of their outstanding keeping qualities. That is to say, they can be hidden away in a dark corner like a reclusive hermit. With their nine-teenth-century roots, these cookies are distinc-tively old-fashioned. I have to say, they're a clear favorite of the old folks in my life. It's a tough race for which platter would empty first at a golden anniversary celebration in my hometown: hermit cookies topped with sugared bourbon, or sliced Gethsemane fruitcake soaked in bourbon.

Makes about 36 cookies

FOR THE COOKIES
½ cup (1 stick) butter, at room temperature
1 cup light brown sugar
2 large eggs
1 tablespoon bourbon
1½ cups all-purpose flour
1 teaspoon baking soda
¼ teaspoon salt
¼ teaspoon ground cinnamon
½ teaspoon ground allspice
¼ teaspoon ground cloves
¾ cup golden raisins
½ cup dried cranberries
¾ cup pitted, chopped dates
1 cup coarsely chopped pecans

FOR THE GLAZE
½ cup confectioners' sugar, sifted
¼ teaspoon pure vanilla extract
¼ teaspoon bourbon
3 tablespoons whole milk, as needed

TO MAKE THE COOKIES

Preheat oven to 350 degrees F. Line two 9 x 13-inch baking sheets with parchment, and set them aside.

In a large mixing bowl, using an electric mixer set on medium-high speed, cream together the butter and brown sugar until light and fluffy, about 3 minutes. Add the eggs, one at a time, beating well after each addition, about 1 minute each. Beat in the bourbon until just blended, about 30 seconds.

In a separate large mixing bowl whisk together the flour, baking soda, salt, cinnamon, allspice, and cloves. A little at a time, add the flour mixture to the butter and egg mixture, and beat after each addition until combined. Using a rubber spatula, fold in the raisins, cranberries, dates, and pecans.

Drop the batter by tablespoons onto the prepared baking sheets, spacing the cookies about two inches apart. Bake for 10 to 12 minutes or until the edges crisp and the tops are lightly browned. Remove from the oven, set the pans on wire racks to cool for about 5 minutes, then transfer the cookies directly onto the rack and let them cool for 10 minutes more.

TO MAKE THE GLAZE

In a small mixing bowl, whisk together the sugar, vanilla, and bourbon.

Add enough milk to make a thick, pourable glaze, about the consistency of pure maple syrup.

Once the cookies are completely cool, use a small spoon to drizzle lines of glaze over each cookie. Let the cookies stand uncovered on a countertop until the glaze has hardened.

Store in the refrigerator, in a cake safe or tin, for up to 1 week.

Bourbon Pineapple-Coconut Squares

During my childhood, the old folks at family gatherings, in my grandmother's home beauty shop, and at church picnics seemed to gravitate toward desserts made with pineapple and coconut. Perhaps it's because these ingredients from the tropical far reaches of the globe were exotic and sophisticated to land-locked Kentuckians born around the turn of the twentieth century. I didn't understand it as a child; I went for the sweetest, most chocolaty desserts on offer. My grown-up palate understands the draw, and begs for a hint of bourbon to go with those not-too-sweet flavors. Note: It's important that this filling be poured into a warm crust. Make the filling first, and set it aside. Right before pouring it onto the crust, give it a quick stir, and you're off to the races.

Makes 40 bars

FOR THE FILLING

6 large eggs, at room temperature
2½ cups granulated sugar
½ cup sweetened shredded coconut flakes
¾ cup pineapple juice
¼ cup bourbon
¾ cup all-purpose flour
¾ teaspoon baking powder
Confectioners' sugar, for garnish
Maraschino cherries, halved, for garnish

FOR THE CRUST

1¾ cups all-purpose flour
⅔ cup confectioners' sugar, plus extra for garnish
¼ cup cornstarch
¾ teaspoon salt
¾ cup (1½ sticks) butter, chilled and cut into
    1-inch pieces, plus more for greasing pan

TO MAKE THE FILLING

In a large mixing bowl, whisk together the eggs, sugar, coconut, pineapple juice, bourbon, flour, and baking powder. Chill this in the refrigerator until the crust is ready.

TO MAKE THE CRUST

Adjust oven rack to middle position and heat oven to 350 degrees F. Lightly butter a 9 x 13-inch baking dish and line with one sheet parchment or wax paper. Dot paper with butter, then lay second sheet crosswise over it.

Sift the flour, confectioners' sugar, cornstarch, and salt into a large mixing bowl, then cut in the butter using a pastry cutter or two butter knives until the mixture resembles a fine meal.

Tip the dough onto a floured surface, and form it into a ball. Transfer the dough into the prepared pan.

Using your floured fingers, press the mixture into an even, ¼-inch layer over the bottom and about ½ inch up sides. Bake the crust until golden brown, about 20 minutes.

Remove from the oven and set the pan on a wire rack to cool for 10 minutes.

TO ASSEMBLE

Take the chilled filling from the refrigerator and stir it with a fork to reblend. Pour the filling onto the crust, and bake for 25 to 30 minutes, until the middle is set.

Remove from the oven and set the pan on a wire rack to cool for 30 minutes. Dust with confectioners' sugar, and cut into squares. Top each with a cherry half, and serve.

Store in the refrigerator, tightly covered with plastic wrap or foil, for up to 5 days.

❧ *Bourbon Fact*

President Lyndon B. Johnson loved him some bourbon: in 1964, he signed an Act of Congress designating bourbon as "The Official Spirit of America," recognizing it as a "Distinctive Product of the U.S."

Cheesecake Bars with Dulce de Leche con Bourbon

Long before the emergence of the Cheesecake Factory, a vogue spread through Louisville of making homemade cheesecake. In the mid-1980s both my grandmother and my mother joined the legions of bridge players and bunko party hostesses and purchased springform pans from the fancy cookware section of Stewart's Dry Goods store. We ate the preliminary failures, and we ate the subsequent successes.

This cake is a much simpler relative, but it yields a delicious result. I updated the idea further by layering on dulce de leche, a rich caramel sauce popular in Latin countries. That may sound worldly, but it simply reminds me of the creamy caramel sauces and frostings my mother loved to top custards and jam cakes with.

Makes 40 bars

FOR THE DULCE DE LECHE
This recipe makes about 1 1/2 cups of dulce de leche, which is more than is needed for the bars. Trust me, once you taste it, you'll want to have a jar on hand. I always make extra when I'm going to the trouble so I'll have it in the fridge to pour over ice cream, stir into custard, or even spread on slices of warm, buttered baguette.

2 (14-ounce) cans sweetened condensed milk (don't confuse this with evaporated milk)
Fleur de sel (or sea salt, kosher salt, even table salt; and experiment with proportions)

FOR THE CRUST
2¼ cups finely crushed graham crackers (from about 17 whole graham crackers)
2 tablespoons sugar
¼ teaspoon ground cinnamon
¾ cup (1½ sticks) unsalted butter, melted, plus more at room temperature for greasing pan

FOR THE FILLING

3 (8-ounce) packages cream cheese,
    room temperature
1 cup granulated sugar
3 large eggs
½ cup dulce de leche
2 teaspoons pure vanilla extract
2 tablespoons bourbon

FOR THE GLAZE

⅔ cup dulce de leche
3 tablespoons (or more) heavy whipping cream
Fleur de sel (or sea salt, kosher salt, even table salt;
    and experiment with proportions)

TO MAKE THE DULCE DE LECHE

Preheat the oven to 425 degrees F.

Pour the sweetened condensed milk into a
2-quart glass baking dish. Sprinkle in ¼ to ½ teaspoon of fleur de sel. Cover the dish snugly with
aluminum foil.

Set the covered dish in a 4-quart glass baking
dish and add hot water until it reaches halfway up
the side.

Bake for about an hour, checking frequently to
add hot water to the bottom dish as it steams off.

After an hour, check the dulce de leche to see if it
is brown enough for your liking. If not, keep baking in 10-minute increments until you're happy.

Once the sauce is nicely browned and caramelized, remove the two dishes from the oven and set
the pan containing the dulce de leche on a wire
rack to cool.

Once the sauce is cool, whisk until it's smooth.

Store in the refrigerator in a tightly lidded jar
or plastic bowl until ready to serve, up to 2 weeks.
Warm gently in a warm water bath or in the microwave oven before using.

TO MAKE THE CRUST

Preheat oven to 350 degrees F.

Butter a 9 x 13-inch metal baking pan.

In a large mixing bowl, use your hands to mix
the graham cracker crumbs, sugar, and cinnamon
until combined.

Add the melted butter, and mix with your
hands until coated.

Pour the crumb mixture into the prepared
pan. Press the crust evenly into the bottom of the
pan, about ¼ inch thick, and about ½ inch up the
sides. Bake until the crust is light golden, about 10
minutes. Remove from the oven and set the pan
on a wire rack to cool for 5 minutes.

TO MAKE THE FILLING

In the bowl of a food processor, pulse the cream cheese and sugar until smooth and creamy, about 3 minutes.

Add the eggs 1 at a time, pulsing about 5 to 10 seconds to combine between additions.

Add the dulce de leche, vanilla, and bourbon, and pulse to combine, about 10 seconds. Chill in the refrigerator until you are ready to assemble.

TO MAKE THE GLAZE

In a medium saucepan, over medium heat, melt the dulce de leche.

Once melted, add the cream, and stir to blend. Keep stirring over the heat until the sauce is a pourable, spreadable consistency, like thick honey. If needed, add more cream, or reduce longer. Remove the glaze from the heat and either store in the refrigerator, or allow to rest if you're assembling the dessert on the spot.

TO BAKE AND ASSEMBLE

When you're ready to bake the bars, spread the filling evenly over the warm crust. (The filling should be at room temperature. If you've made it ahead and refrigerated it, allow it to rest on the counter for 10 minutes.)

Bake at 350 degrees F until just set in center and edges are puffed, slightly cracked, and pulling away from the sides of the pan, about 35 to 40 minutes. Remove from the oven, set the pan on a wire rack, and cool completely.

Once cooled, pour the glaze over the cooled cheesecake, and spread it evenly using a rubber spatula dipped in water. Refrigerate until chilled, about 1 hour.

Cut into bars, sprinkle with fleur de sel, and serve.

Store in the refrigerator, tightly covered with plastic wrap or foil, for up to 5 days.

Warm and Spicy Bourbon Chocolate Chip Cookie Bars

⟩ These bars remind me of the Congo bars beloved of southern bakers of a certain age (like my mother!), made popular by the fact that they'd weather mailing in care packages to Korean War soldiers. But I'll warn you: these toothsome bars are not your grandma's toll house cookies! With the multi-note flavors of oaky bourbon, warm winter spices, and dark, earthy chocolate, these treats demand a drink that can stand up to their boldness. Why not serve them with an espresso garnished with a lemon peel, accompanied by a shot of the very bourbon that boosted their sophistication quotient into the stratosphere?

Makes 32 bars

2¼ cups flour
1 heaping tablespoon finely grated fresh ginger (or use 1 teaspoon ground ginger)
½ teaspoon ground cinnamon
¼ teaspoon ground cloves
1 teaspoon baking soda
½ teaspoon salt
1 cup (2 sticks) unsalted butter, at room temperature, plus more for greasing pan
1¼ cups granulated sugar
1¼ cups light brown sugar
4 eggs
3 tablespoons bourbon
12 ounces dark chocolate chips

Preheat the oven to 350 degrees F. Butter a 9 x 13-inch glass baking pan.

In a large mixing bowl, whisk together the flour, ginger, cinnamon, cloves, baking soda, and salt.

In a separate large mixing bowl, using an electric beater, cream together the butter, granulated sugar, and brown sugar until light and fluffy, about 3 minutes.

Add the eggs, one at a time, beating well after each, about 45 seconds. Gradually add the bourbon, mixing at a low speed until blended, about 1 minute.

Add the flour mixture, a little at a time, mixing until just blended. Using a spatula, fold in the chocolate chips, and mix to combine.

Spread the batter evenly into the prepared pan, and bake until wooden cake tester or metal skewer inserted in the center comes out clean, about 45 minutes.

Remove from the oven, set the pan on a wire rack, and cool for 30 minutes. Cut into bars and serve.

Store in a cake safe or airtight tin for up to 1 week.

Buttery Bourbon-Oatmeal Cookies

It's my assertion that oatmeal cookies are hands down the safest bet of the cookie world. I have never once heard a human—man, woman, or child—utter the words, "No, I don't like oatmeal cookies!" Okay, I exaggerate, but I think most people agree that oatmeal cookies of any stripe are sure crowd pleasers. The bourbon in this recipe adds a deep, woodsy note that complements the earthy oats perfectly, giving these cookies extra presence.

Makes about 2 dozen cookies

½ cup dried cherries
¾ cup bourbon, for soaking cherries
½ cup granulated sugar
¼ cup dark brown sugar
½ cup (1 stick) butter, at room temperature
¾ teaspoon pure vanilla extract
3 tablespoons bourbon
1 large egg, at room temperature
½ cup all-purpose flour
1½ cups rolled oats
¼ cup almond flour (see page 14)
½ teaspoon baking powder
½ teaspoon baking soda

At least one day, and up to two weeks, in advance, combine the dried cherries and the bourbon in a tightly lidded jar. Shake the jar briskly from time to time to infuse.

Preheat oven to 350 degrees F. Line two 9 x 13-inch baking sheets with parchment.

Using an electric mixer set on medium-high speed, cream together the granulated sugar, brown sugar, butter, vanilla, and bourbon. Beat until light and fluffy, about 3 minutes. Add the egg, and beat for 1 minute more.

In a large mixing bowl, whisk together the flour, oats, almond flour, baking powder, and baking soda and add it to the butter mixture a little at a time, beating between additions to combine, about 1 minute for each addition.

Drain the dried cherries, reserving the liquid to sip straight or use in cocktails. Add the drained cherries to the batter, and beat until just combined, less than 1 minute.

Drop the batter by tablespoons, leaving about 2 inches between the cookies.

Bake for 10 to 12 minutes, or until golden brown.

Remove from the oven, set the baking sheets on wire racks, and cool for 5 minutes, then transfer the cookies directly to the racks.

Store in a cake safe or airtight tin for up to 10 days.

Kentucky Plus

> For Thanksgiving cookies, substitute dried cranberries for the cherries.

> For a version of Kitchen Sink Cookies, stir in ⅓ cup macadamia nuts, ⅓ cup dark chocolate chips, ⅓ cup whole peanuts, and ⅓ cup raisins.

> Frost with Bourbon and Sorghum Buttercream (page 140), made by swapping out the sorghum with pure maple syrup in equal parts.

Boilermaker Brownies

Some purists maintain that a boilermaker is a mug of beer with a shot of bourbon back. Others insist that a shot glass of whiskey must be "depth-charged" into the mug of beer and the contents downed in one breath to qualify. Either way, the drinker winds up with two excellent beverages: beer and whiskey. I think the old men sitting at the long, wooden bars in the Louisville neighborhoods close to downtown used to order boilermakers because they simply couldn't choose one over the other. Add chocolate, and it's hard to want for anything else, except maybe a racing sheet and a long stretch of Saturday afternoon where you're not expected anyplace. It won't shock you to hear that these brownies go down nice and smooth with a pint of Kentucky Bourbon Barrel Ale.

Makes 36 brownies

1 cup all-purpose flour
¼ cup unsweetened cocoa powder (I like Scharffen Berger's)
½ teaspoon salt
8 ounces dark chocolate (80% cacao), chopped
½ cup (1 stick) butter, plus 1 tablespoon for greasing pan
4 large eggs, at room temperature
1 cup dark brown sugar, packed
½ cup granulated sugar
1 teaspoon pure vanilla extract
¾ cup dark stout (I like Kentucky Breakfast Stout), at room temperature
¼ cup bourbon
1 cup semisweet chocolate chips

Preheat oven to 350 degrees F. Butter a 9 x 13-inch glass baking dish.

In a large mixing bowl, whisk together the flour, cocoa powder, and salt until combined; set aside.

Meanwhile, melt the chocolate and butter together in a double boiler, over low heat, stirring constantly until melted. Remove it from the heat, and set it aside.

In a large mixing bowl, using an electric beater set on medium-high speed, cream together the eggs, brown sugar, and granulated sugar until light and fluffy, about 3 minutes.

A little at a time, add the melted chocolate mixture, and beat until combined after each addition.

Gradually add the flour mixture, and beat until smooth, about 3 minutes.

Add the vanilla, stout, and bourbon and stir in with a fork until smooth. (The batter might seem thin, but don't worry.)

Pour the batter into the prepared baking dish, then sprinkle the chocolate chips evenly over the top of the batter.

Bake in the center of the oven for 35 minutes, or until the edges crisp and pull away from the pan and a wooden cake tester or metal skewer inserted in the middle comes out clean.

Remove from the oven, set the pan on a wire rack to cool for 30 minutes, then cut into squares and serve.

Store in a cake safe or airtight tin for up to 2 weeks.

Bourbon and Spice Gingersnaps

⤜ Back in the day, when Jefferson County schools in my hometown of Louisville were closed for a snow day, everyone headed out to Cherokee Park or the hill behind the Baptist Seminary to sled. In the era before Gore-tex and the Internet, the five kids in my family passed around rubber army boots stocked in a variety of sizes and hand-crocheted scarves and toboggan caps made by my grandmother. In the rush to leave the house, it wasn't unusual to wind up with one glove and one mitten. We kids didn't care. The excitement was so great, we didn't feel the cold.

These cookies, with their winter spices and bourbon flavor, are just the thing to offer your returning crew of dedicated Radio Flyer pilots.

Makes about 3 dozen gingersnaps

1 cup granulated sugar, plus more for
    coating dough
1 medium egg
¼ teaspoon salt
¾ cup (1½ sticks) butter, at room temperature
2 cups all-purpose flour
½ teaspoon baking soda
2 teaspoons peeled and grated fresh ginger
1 teaspoon ground ginger
1 teaspoon ground cloves
1 teaspoon ground cinnamon
2 tablespoons bourbon

Preheat the oven to 350 degrees F. Line three 9 x 13-inch baking sheets with parchment. Fill a small bowl with sugar for coating dough, and set it aside.

In a large mixing bowl, using an electric mixer set on high speed, cream together the sugar, egg, salt, and butter until light and creamy, about 3 minutes.

In a separate mixing bowl, whisk together the flour, baking soda, fresh ginger, ground ginger, cloves, cinnamon, and bourbon.

Add the dry mixture to the wet mixture a little at a time and beat until it's fully mixed, taking care not to overwork it.

Using lightly floured hands, roll the dough into balls about the size of a large grape; then roll the balls in the sugar and place them on the prepared baking sheets, about 2 inches apart. Bake for 6 to 8 minutes, or until browned on top, and crispy at the edges.

Remove from the oven, transfer the cookies onto wire cooling racks, and cool slightly before serving, or allow them to cool completely and store in an airtight container for up to a month.

3   Pies, Tarts, and Cobblers

Where I come from, a hot fruit dessert adorned with a high-rise crust made from a simple batter is commonly referred to as a cobbler. Different versions are known as crisps, crumbles, slumps, and grunts. The thing all of these economical and simple-to-prepare goodies have in common is their mission to use what needs to be used up. Sometimes, that's bushels of fruit gleaned from seasonal trees and bushes. Sometimes, making a cobbler means the final Hail Mary for fruit that won't last the night, pressing what's on its last legs into action. The reasons for concocting these satisfying desserts that almost eat like meals fall away once the fruited pastry is in the oven or on the stove. It's hard to question the whys and wherefores of the life of a piece of fruit when your mouth is full of warm, jammy pastry.

The fruit creations in this chapter are the ones that lend themselves to the addition of warm, mellow bourbon. I hope you'll immerse yourself in the richness of the spirit layered on top of what are doubtless versions of your grandmothers', mother's, and aunts' signature dishes.

Nutty Bourbon Fudge No-Crust Pie

This easy-to-make dessert is a favorite of my kids. It's good at any temperature. Cold from the fridge, it's like fudge. At room temperature, it's like a brownie. Warmed slightly and topped with vanilla ice cream, it's like uber-deluxe hot fudge cake. As expected as a simple chocolate dessert can be, this one never disappoints. The splash of bourbon lends a distinctive flavor and a unique aroma, making it so much more than your basic bar or brownie.

Makes one 10-inch pie

½ cup (1 stick) butter, plus 1 tablespoon for greasing pan
1 cup bittersweet chocolate chips
¾ cup light brown sugar, packed
2 large eggs, plus 2 large egg yolks
1 teaspoon vanilla
2 tablespoons bourbon
¼ cup all-purpose flour
¼ teaspoon salt
¾ cup chopped walnuts

Preheat the oven to 325 degrees F. Butter a 10-inch pie plate.

In a large, heat-proof mixing bowl, melt the butter and chocolate in the microwave, stirring several times during the process. Once it melts, set it aside.

Using an electric mixer set on medium speed, beat the sugar into the butter mixture until smooth, about 3 minutes.

Add the eggs, egg yolks, vanilla, and bourbon and mix well with a fork. Stir in the flour and salt just to combine; then fold in the walnuts.

Pour the mixture into the prepared pan, and smooth the top with a rubber spatula dipped in water.

Bake for 18 to 20 minutes, just until the center is set and the edges crisp and begin to pull away from the pan.

Remove from the oven, set the pan on a wire rack, and cool for 20 minutes. Serve warm, or store in the refrigerator, tightly covered with plastic wrap or foil, for up to 5 days.

How to Make Bourbon Whipped Cream

Here's how I like to make bourbon whipped cream. If I'm making it to accompany an already very-sweet treat, I leave out the sugar. But never the bourbon . . .

1 cup heavy cream, very cold
½ teaspoon granulated sugar
¼ teaspoon pure vanilla extract
1 tablespoon bourbon

In a large metal mixing bowl, combine the cream, sugar, vanilla, and bourbon, and refrigerate for at least 15 minutes. Stick the beaters of your mixer in the fridge too, while you're at it.

With the electric mixer set to high speed, beat until soft peaks form when the beater is raised, or until the cream mounds softly when dropped from a spoon. Do not overbeat, or you'll wind up with a stiff, dry substance that's a little like butter.

Store in the refrigerator for up to 2 days, but it's best when made and used on the spot.

Gingery Pear and Bourbon Tart

⟫ I only learned recently that pears don't ripen on the tree, like some fruits. Rather, you have to wait patiently, which explains the many hard, flavorless pears I've bitten into and tossed out over the years.

I didn't understand it at the time, but this is why there were heavy-duty beer bottle boxes stuffed with newspaper-wrapped pears in our basement. You knew they were there because of the fragrance. I later found out that they were picked and hand-wrapped by my mother and older brothers at Huber's Orchard, across the bridge that traverses the Ohio River to Indiana.

Store your pears in paper bags, and only make this tart once they're pliant, with a sweet, fruity aroma.

This sweet pastry dough coupled with a shot of good bourbon and some fresh ginger showcases the humble fruit in an elegant way.

Makes one 9-inch tart

FOR THE CRUST

1 cup all-purpose flour
2 tablespoons sugar
Pinch of salt
6 tablespoons (¾ stick) very cold unsalted butter, cut in pieces
1 large egg
1 tablespoon lemon juice or cold water
1 tablespoon bourbon

FOR THE FILLING

4 medium, very ripe pears
1 large egg
3 tablespoons light molasses
1 cup heavy cream
2 tablespoons grated ginger

TO MAKE THE CRUST

In the bowl of a food processor combine the flour, sugar, salt, and butter. Pulse for 3 or 4 short bursts, just until the butter resembles small, sandy marbles.

Add the egg, lemon juice, and bourbon, and process just until the dough starts to stick to the blades, about 1 minute.

Turn the dough out onto a very lightly floured surface, and form into a ball. Put the dough ball in a bowl, cover it tightly, and chill for around 2 hours in the refrigerator.

On a lightly floured surface, roll the dough out into a circle about ¼ inch thick, a little larger than a 9-inch pie plate. Lay the dough over the pie plate, and gently press it down using your fingertips, taking care not to stretch or overwork it. Trim the dough, and crimp the edge. Cover the crust lightly and chill for 30 minutes.

TO MAKE THE FILLING

Preheat the oven to 350 degrees F.

Peel and core the pears, and halve them lengthwise. Slice the halves lengthwise, in thin slices, about ⅛ inch thick. Remove the crust from the refrigerator, and lay the pears inside the crust, with the stem ends in the middle. Your goal is to cover the entire bottom of the tart. Cut slices into smaller pieces to fill in any gaps. Set the tart on a baking sheet.

In a small mixing bowl, combine the egg and molasses, then stir in the cream a little at a time until it's well blended.

TO ASSEMBLE

Pour the egg-cream mixture over the pears, taking care not to overfill. Sprinkle the ginger on top, distributing it evenly (it will sink).

Bake until the crust is golden brown, the pears become tender, and the custard sets up in the middle, about 40 minutes. Remove the pie plate to a wire rack and cool for at least an hour before serving.

Store leftovers in the refrigerator, tightly covered with plastic wrap or foil, for up to 3 days.

Kentucky Plus

- Substitute 5 cooking apples for the pears (I suggest Cortland, Braeburn, or Jonagold), and swap out the ginger for 1½ teaspoons ground cinnamon.

- If pears are out of season, use 8 canned pear halves.

Strawberry-Rhubarb Slab Pie with Vanilla-Bourbon Icing

Oh, the forgiving joy of a slab piecrust! I frequently hear from newbie bakers that they've never made a pie and are wowed by those who dare to. I tell them to get their feet wet with this one. Make it in the summertime, when the rhubarb is abundant in Kentucky backyards and strawberries are as cheap as kittens. Then reward your bravery by throwing bourbon into the frosting.

Makes about 2 dozen squares

FOR THE PIE

3¼ cups all-purpose flour, plus more for
    work surface
1 teaspoon salt
1 cup (2 sticks) butter
¾ cup whole milk, plus more, as needed
1 egg yolk
2 cups granulated sugar
⅓ cup cornstarch
5 cups strawberries, cut into quarters
3 cups rhubarb, cut into ½-inch chunks
Bourbon, for sprinkling

FOR THE ICING

1¼ cups confectioners' sugar
1 tablespoon bourbon
3 tablespoons whole milk, more or less as needed

In a large mixing bowl, combine flour and salt. Using a pastry cutter or two butter knives, cut in the butter until you have coarse crumbs.

In a separate large mixing bowl, whisk together ¾ cup milk and egg yolk until blended. Gradually add the milk and egg mixture to the flour mixture, stirring with a fork until dough forms a ball. If needed, add additional milk, a tablespoon at a time.

Turn the dough out onto a surface and divide it in half (you'll be making top and bottom crusts). One of the halves should be slightly larger than the other. Flatten each half to about an inch thick, wrap each in plastic wrap, and chill in the refrigerator for 1 hour.

Tear off four sheets of waxed paper. Lay one out on the countertop and sprinkle it with flour. Remove the larger portion of the dough from the refrigerator.

Lay the dough onto the waxed paper, sprinkle it with flour, and lay another sheet of waxed paper on top. Roll out dough until you have about a 12 x 16-inch rectangle.

Transfer rolled-out dough to an ungreased 9 x 13-inch baking sheet. Press the dough onto the bottom and up the sides of pan, overhanging slightly by about ½ inch to 1 inch.

Preheat the oven to 375 degrees F.

In a large bowl, combine the sugar and cornstarch. Add the strawberries and rhubarb. Using a spatula, toss to coat. Sprinkle on a teaspoon or two of bourbon to help melt the sugar and add flavor. Ladle the filling into the bottom crust.

Sprinkle another sheet of waxed paper with flour, and remove the remaining dough from the refrigerator. Sprinkle the dough with flour, and lay another sheet of waxed paper on top. Roll it out to about a 9 x 13-inch rectangle, and lay it on top of the filling. Fold the bottom pastry over edge of top pastry edge, and pinch it together. Using a fork, make about 6 pricks in the top to vent.

Bake for 45 to 55 minutes, or until golden brown. Remove from the oven and set the pan on a wire rack to cool.

In a medium-sized mixing bowl, combine the confectioners' sugar and bourbon and whisk until smooth. Add enough milk so that the icing has a drizzling consistency, like warm honey. Drizzle icing evenly over the cooled pie. Cut into squares, and serve.

Store in the refrigerator, tightly covered with plastic or foil, for up to 5 days.

❧ *Bourbon Fact*

Fall is the time to get your drink on: in 2007, the U.S. Senate declared September to be Bourbon Heritage Month.

Grandma Rose's Big Race Pie

One of the most famous Kentucky desserts is the Derby Pie®, purportedly created by George Kern and his parents nearly half a century ago. It became the signature pastry of the Melrose Inn in Prospect, Kentucky, and was such a success that the Kerns obtained a trademark for it in 1968, the year I attended my very first Derby Party.

My grandmother had a huge smile, and giggled like a schoolgirl when she was tickled. One of the most precious gifts of my life is that she delighted in me. She taught me to cook, never caring that I slopped batter from the bowl or measured without accuracy. She'd stand back and watch, just letting me "do." I have fond memories of being allowed to dump in the chocolate chips for this pie, splashing the batter as I did. And of her watching me do it, tickled and giggling.

Makes one 9-inch pie

FOR THE CRUST
1½ cups all-purpose flour
¼ teaspoon salt
1 teaspoon granulated sugar
½ cup (1 stick) cold butter, cut into small pieces
4 to 5 tablespoons ice water

FOR THE FILLING
¼ cup (½ stick) butter, softened
1 cup of sugar
3 large eggs
¾ cup white Karo syrup
½ teaspoon salt
2 teaspoons vanilla
2 tablespoons bourbon
½ cup chopped pecans
1 cup semisweet chocolate chips

TO MAKE THE CRUST
Combine the flour, salt, and sugar in a large mixing bowl and whisk to combine and aerate. Using a pastry cutter or two butter knives, blend in the butter until the mixture resembles small, sandy marbles, about 4 to 5 minutes.

Add 4 tablespoons of ice water and mix with a fork, just until the dough comes together. (Add the last tablespoon of ice water if needed, but don't overwork the dough or it'll become tough.)

Shape the dough into a flat disk, cover it in plastic wrap, and refrigerate it for an hour (or for up to 2 days, if you'd like to make it in advance).

Remove the dough from the refrigerator, and roll it out with a rolling pin on a lightly floured surface into a 12-inch circle, about ⅛ inch thick. As you roll, if the dough is sticking to the surface below, sprinkle a small amount of flour under the dough to keep the dough from sticking.

Line the dough circle up above a 9-inch pie plate, then gently press down so that it lines the bottom and sides of the plate. Use kitchen scissors to trim the dough to within ½ inch of the edge of the pie dish, then crimp it with your fingers.

TO MAKE THE FILLING
In a large mixing bowl, using an electric mixer set on medium-high speed, cream the butter and sugar together about 5 minutes. Add the eggs one at a time, beating to combine after each, about 30 to 45 seconds.

Add the syrup, salt, vanilla, and bourbon, and beat until just combined, about 2 minutes. Add the pecans and chocolate chips, and fold them in using a rubber spatula.

TO ASSEMBLE AND BAKE
Preheat the oven to 375 degrees F.

Place the unbaked crust onto a baking sheet. Pour in the filling.

Bake 40 to 50 minutes or until the middle is set and the crust is golden brown. Remove the entire pan to a wire cooling rack and cool for at least an hour before serving, or it will be runny and won't slice right.

Store in a cake safe or airtight tin for up to 1 week.

Bourbon and Buttermilk Pie in a Cream Cheese Crust

A true Kentucky specialty, this dairy-rich pie is a typical and delicious example of the kind of custard pie we southerners love. In the family of the chess pie, it's also a country cousin of the cottage cheese pie.

The dough for this piecrust must be made a day in advance. I think this filling and piecrust combination taste special together, but if you use a regular store-bought piecrust in a pinch, you'll still have a real rootsy, down-home pie that'll conjure up happy childhood memories and satisfied sighs from the Kentucky-born elder statesmen at your table.

Makes one 9-inch pie

FOR THE CRUST

1 cup all-purpose flour
1 tablespoon confectioners' sugar
⅛ teaspoon baking powder
½ cup (1 stick) salted butter, at room temperature
4 ounces (½ package) full-fat cream cheese, at room temperature
½ teaspoon vanilla

FOR THE FILLING

3 large eggs, at room temperature
¾ cup sugar
3 tablespoons all-purpose flour
1½ cups buttermilk
½ teaspoon pure vanilla extract
2 tablespoons bourbon
1 tablespoon lemon juice
1 tablespoon lemon zest (from 1 medium-sized lemon)
3 tablespoons butter, melted
Ground cinnamon, for dusting
Freshly grated nutmeg, for dusting

TO MAKE THE CRUST

Preheat the oven to 400 degrees F.

In a large mixing bowl, sift together the flour, confectioners' sugar, and baking powder. Set aside.

In a separate large mixing bowl, using an electric mixer, cream together the butter, cream cheese, and vanilla until light and fluffy, about 3 minutes.

Add the butter mixture to the dry ingredients a little at a time, using your hands. Crumble it together with your fingers until it resembles small marbles in sand, about 3 or 4 minutes.

Turn the dough out onto a clean, lightly floured surface and blend it well, using the heels of your hands. Press the dough into a ball, wrap in plastic wrap, and refrigerate overnight.

The next day, roll the dough out on a clean, lightly floured surface using as little extra flour as you can possibly get away with while achieving a thin crust. The thinness of the crust is important because this recipe contains baking powder, which will lift and aerate it.

Lay the crust over a 9-inch pie pan, then press it down, crimp the edges, and prick it all over with a fork.

Bake the crust until done, but not golden-brown, about 10 minutes. Remove from the oven, set on a wire rack, and cool for at least 15 minutes before adding the filling.

TO MAKE THE FILLING

Reduce the oven temperature to 375 degrees F.

In a large mixing bowl, using an electric mixer, beat the eggs and sugar together. When fluffy and bright yellow in color, add the flour and beat again, about 3 to 4 minutes.

Add the buttermilk and mix to combine, about 1 minute. Then add the vanilla, bourbon, lemon juice, lemon zest, and butter, and mix again, about 1 minute more.

Pour the mixture into the cooled piecrust, and lightly dust the surface with a small amount of cinnamon, followed by a small amount of nutmeg. (Hint: You should still see plenty of yellow pie filling beneath the spices.)

Bake for 20 to 30 minutes, or until the filling is just set in the middle and the crust is golden brown.

Remove from the oven, set on a wire rack, and allow it to rest for an hour before serving.

Store in the refrigerator, tightly covered with plastic wrap or foil, for up to 5 days.

✌ Bourbon Fact

My Old Brooklyn Home?

It's a myth that all bourbon is from Kentucky. Under U.S. law, spirits called bourbon must only be made in the United States. In fact, 95 percent of bourbon sold today is manufactured in Kentucky, but it's also made in Indiana, Iowa, Massachusetts, and even New York City!

Bourbon–Sour Cream Apple Pie with Crumb Topping

⟐ I'm an American, so I guess I have to say I like apple pie. I don't pass it up, but I don't really go looking for it. This version, however, has captured my fancy. The tang of the sour cream takes the bite out of the apples' tartness. And the crumb topping is almost like eating candied nuts. The bourbon, though, is what kicks this up into the "must have" category for me. I like it for a summer picnic to go with cold fried chicken and potato salad, or as a fall dessert after an evening meal of roast chicken.

Makes one 10-inch pie

FOR THE CRUST
1¾ cups all-purpose flour
¼ cup sugar
1 teaspoon cinnamon
½ teaspoon salt
½ cup plus 2 tablespoons (1¼ sticks) butter, cold
¼ cup apple cider, cold

FOR THE FILLING
8 medium Winesap or McIntosh apples, peeled, cored, and sliced
1⅔ cups full-fat sour cream
1 cup sugar
⅓ cup all-purpose flour
1 egg
3 teaspoons bourbon
1 teaspoon pure vanilla extract
½ teaspoon salt

FOR THE TOPPING
1 cup chopped walnuts
½ cup all-purpose flour
⅓ cup dark brown sugar, packed
⅓ cup granulated sugar
2 teaspoons cinnamon
Pinch of salt
½ cup (1 stick) butter, room temperature

TO MAKE THE CRUST
In a medium-sized mixing bowl, combine the flour, sugar, cinnamon, and salt. Cut in the butter using a pastry cutter or two butter knives until the mixture looks like small, sandy pebbles.

Add the cider and mix gently with a fork until combined. Gather the dough into a ball, and transfer it to a lightly floured surface.

Roll the dough into a circle slightly larger than a deep 10-inch pie plate, about ¼ inch thick. Line the crust up over the plate and press it in, crimping a thick, high rim at the edge. Set aside.

TO MAKE THE FILLING

Preheat the oven to 450 degrees F.

Combine the apples, sour cream, sugar, flour, egg, bourbon, vanilla, and salt in a large bowl and mix well using a rubber spatula.

Ladle the filling into the crust, and bake for 10 minutes.

Reduce oven temperature to 350 degrees F and continue baking until the filling is set up in the middle and golden brown on top, about 40 minutes. (If the crust is browning too quickly, shield the crust only with aluminum foil.)

TO MAKE THE TOPPING

While the crust and filling bake, combine the walnuts, flour, brown sugar, granulated sugar, cinnamon, and salt in medium-sized mixing bowl, and stir with a fork to combine. Using your hands, blend in the butter until mixture resembles coarse crumbs.

Spoon the topping over pie, and bake for 15 minutes more, until brown.

Remove from the oven and set on a wire rack to cool for an hour before serving.

Store in the refrigerator, tightly covered with plastic wrap or foil, for up to 5 days.

Cornbread Apple-Raisin Cobbler with a Splash of Bourbon

Cobblers are a winner every time because they're easy, and they make use of what's on hand. No wonder they're a staple of country folk and farmers. Practical and delicious, they evoke memories of a warm, homey kitchen in every person I know. Did you eat cobbler at a cabin by the river? When you went to visit "your people" in the country? When your mom was making the most of the last apples in the cellar?

However you remember it, I think that this quintessential Kentucky version with cornbread and bourbon will please you and warm your heart.

Makes one 8 x 8-inch cobbler

FOR THE FILLING

5 large Granny Smith apples, peeled, cored, and sliced thinly
½ cup raisins
¼ cup bourbon
¼ cup packed dark brown sugar
1 tablespoon all-purpose flour
½ teaspoon ground cinnamon
½ teaspoon ground nutmeg
¼ teaspoon ground cardamom

FOR THE CORNBREAD CRUST

1 cup cornmeal
1 cup all-purpose flour
¼ cup dark brown sugar, packed
1 tablespoon baking powder
1 teaspoon salt
½ cup whole milk
½ cup plain whole-milk yogurt
¼ cup extra virgin olive oil
1 large egg

TO MAKE THE FILLING

Preheat the oven to 400 degrees F. Lightly butter an 8 by 8-inch glass baking dish.

In a medium-sized mixing bowl, combine the apples, raisins, bourbon, brown sugar, flour, cinnamon, nutmeg, and cardamom. Toss with a fork to thoroughly coat the apples, and pour the mixture into the prepared baking dish.

TO MAKE THE CORNBREAD CRUST

In a large mixing bowl, whisk together the cornmeal, flour, brown sugar, baking powder, and salt. In a separate small bowl, whisk together the milk, yogurt, olive oil, and egg. Add the egg mixture to the cornmeal mixture, and fold together with a spatula until the mixture is just incorporated.

TO ASSEMBLE AND BAKE

Spoon the cornbread crust on top of the fruit filling. Bake for about 30 to 35 minutes, until the filling is bubbly and the cornbread topping is golden. Serve warm from the oven. Store leftovers in the dish, tightly covered with plastic wrap or foil, for up to 5 days.

Kentucky Plus

- Substitute 6 fresh peaches, peeled and pitted, and leave out the cinnamon and nutmeg for a summery peach cobbler.

- If it's blackberry season, use 4 cups blackberries instead of the apples, and leave out the raisins, cinnamon, nutmeg, and cardamom. Switch the brown sugar to white granulated sugar.

Pumpkin-Bourbon Tart with Nutty Cinnamon Streusel

⤳ Pumpkin is one of my favorite flavors, and each year I delight in the appearance of pumpkin ice cream, pumpkin pie spiced coffee, pumpkin doughnuts, and pumpkin muffins at the various markets, coffee houses, and bakeries in my neighborhood.

This tart is all that, plus. Elegant to look at, it makes a nice centerpiece to an autumn dinner party. The bourbon gives it a worldly feel, like something you'd be offered in a restaurant with leather chairs and heavy deep wood paneling. And let me tell you a secret: men love it.

Makes one 9-inch tart

FOR THE CRUST
2 cups all-purpose flour
⅓ cup sugar
½ teaspoon salt
⅔ cup (1¼ sticks) butter, cold, and cut into pieces
1 large egg, lightly beaten
¼ cup heavy cream

FOR THE FILLING
1 (15-ounce) can packed pumpkin (not pie filling)
3 eggs
½ cup sugar
½ cup heavy cream
¼ cup dark brown sugar, packed
¼ cup bourbon
2 tablespoons all-purpose flour
½ teaspoon ground cinnamon
2 teaspoons finely chopped fresh ginger
¼ teaspoon salt
¼ teaspoon ground cloves

FOR THE TOPPING
¾ cup all-purpose flour
⅓ cup sugar
⅓ cup dark brown sugar, packed
½ teaspoon salt
1½ teaspoons ground cinnamon
½ cup (1 stick) butter, cold, cut into pieces
¾ cup coarsely chopped walnuts

TO MAKE THE CRUST

In a large mixing bowl, combine the flour, sugar, and salt. Cut in butter until crumbly. Add egg. Gradually add cream, tossing with a fork until a ball forms. Cover and refrigerate for at least 30 minutes or until easy to handle.

TO MAKE THE FILLING

In a large mixing bowl, combine the pumpkin, eggs, sugar, cream, brown sugar, bourbon, flour, cinnamon, ginger, salt, and cloves. Gently fold together using a rubber spatula until smooth. Set aside in the refrigerator.

TO MAKE THE TOPPING

In a medium-sized mixing bowl, combine the flour, granulated sugar, brown sugar, salt, and cinnamon, and whisk until blended and aerated. Using a pastry cutter or two butter knives, cut in the butter until the mixture looks like small, sandy marbles. Gently stir in the walnuts and ginger. Set aside.

TO ASSEMBLE AND BAKE

Preheat the oven to 350 degrees F. Position an ungreased 9-inch fluted tart pan with a removable bottom on a baking sheet. Remove the dough from the refrigerator, and roll out into about an 11-inch circle on a lightly floured surface. Line up the dough circle over the tart pan and press it into the bottom and up the sides. Ladle the filling into the crust.

Evenly distribute the topping over the filling.

Bake 45 to 55 minutes or until a wooden cake tester or metal skewer inserted into the middle comes out clean. Remove from the oven, set on a wire rack, and cool for 30 minutes before serving.

Store leftovers in the pie plate, tightly covered with plastic wrap or foil, for up to 5 days.

Cast-Iron Skillet Sour Cherry and Bourbon Slump

Sour cherry trees have proven to successfully and reliably yield abundant fruit in Kentucky. My mother had memories of her dad returning from the family farm out in the country laden with the garnet fruit.

Because sour cherries feel old-fashioned to me, I love to use them in this slump, cooked in an iron skillet. A slump, like its relative the cobbler, is one of those easy-to-whip-up treats that make use of what's around. Made entirely on the stove top, it was likely a favorite in the days before air conditioning, when people avoided "heating up the kitchen." Plan on making this, and then serving it fresh and warm right away. My advice is to have plenty of vanilla ice cream and some Bourbon Whipped Cream (page 71) standing at the ready.

Makes one 9-inch slump

FOR THE TOPPING
1 cup all-purpose flour
2 tablespoons sugar, plus more for topping
1 teaspoon baking powder
¼ teaspoon baking soda
¼ teaspoon salt
2 tablespoons butter, melted
½ cup full-fat sour cream

FOR THE FILLING
2 pints sour cherries, pitted
½ cup dark brown sugar, packed
3 tablespoons granulated sugar
¼ cup bourbon
1 tablespoon lemon juice
Zest of 1 lemon
¼ teaspoon salt

TO MAKE THE TOPPING
In a large mixing bowl, whisk together the flour, sugar, baking powder, baking soda, and salt until blended and aerated.

Using a rubber spatula, stir in the melted butter and mix until combined.

Add half the sour cream and stir again. Working a little at a time, add the remaining sour cream, stirring between additions, until a wet dough forms. Set the dough aside in the refrigerator.

TO MAKE THE FILLING

In a well-seasoned 9-inch cast-iron skillet, combine the cherries, brown sugar, granulated sugar, bourbon, lemon juice, lemon zest, and salt.

Cover with a tight-fitting lid or with two layers of aluminum foil, and bring the mixture to a rolling boil over medium heat.

When the mixture reaches a boil, remove the skillet from the heat and scoop heaping tablespoons of the biscuit topping over the cherries, covering as much surface area as possible.

Sprinkle the top of the dough with sugar.

Cover tightly and return the pan to the burner, over low heat. Cook 20 minutes, without uncovering. After 20 minutes, check for doneness. The slump is done when the topping is dry to the touch (it will not brown).

Serve the slump hot from the pan.

Store in the refrigerator in a tightly lidded plastic bowl for up to 1 week.

Inside-Out Bourbon-Apple Crisp

This dessert is a showpiece that tastes as good as it looks. Each apple cup holds a nutty oatmeal crisp mixture, moistened with bourbon, so it offers a wide variety of appealing flavors and textures. I'd say this dessert is great for the health conscious, but I'd be a hypocrite. These beauties never leave my kitchen without the à la mode treatment.

Makes 6 individual desserts

6 large Pink Lady apples (you can substitute Gala or Honeycrisp)
⅔ cup oats
¾ cup loosely packed brown sugar
¼ cup plus 1 tablespoon flour
1 teaspoon cinnamon
½ teaspoon allspice
½ teaspoon salt
¼ cup (½ stick) butter, at room temperature
1 teaspoon pure vanilla extract
½ cup finely ground walnuts
1 cup apple cider
⅓ cup bourbon

Preheat the oven to 400 degrees F. Spray a 9 x 13-inch glass baking dish with nonstick spray.

Using an apple corer, cut about three-fourths of the way down into the middle of each apple. Remove all of the core and the seeds, but leave a "bottom" to the bowl you'll make of the partially hollowed-out apple. Using a paring knife, widen the hole at the top, cutting about an inch downward. This gives extra space to hold the stuffing.

In a medium-sized mixing bowl, combine the oats, brown sugar, flour, cinnamon, allspice, and salt. Stir with a fork until blended.

Add the softened butter and vanilla, and mix thoroughly with a fork until a clumpy batter forms.

Add the walnuts, and stir again. Stuff the apples with the mixture, dividing evenly among the 6 apples.

Arrange the apples in the prepared baking dish. Pour the apple cider and bourbon into the bottom of the pan, and bake for 45 minutes, basting the apples every 10 minutes with the apple-bourbon syrup from the pan. The apples are done when the skin wrinkles and they begin to brown and crisp. Remove the pan from the oven, and serve immediately.

Store in the refrigerator in a tightly lidded plastic bowl for up to 1 week. Reheat in the oven or microwave before serving.

4   Puddings, Trifles, and Custards

Creamy, lush, spoonable desserts from the pudding, trifle, and custard family are the ones most likely to transport us home. Most include rich dairy and lots of sugar, strong features of childhood fare.

These are the foods that were fed to us by worried bedside mothers when we were under the weather, or given to us prior to a long winter's nap to smooth away the cares of the day and prepare us to lay our heads on our pillows.

As basic as these desserts are, their elegance is evident. Most are not out of place on a linen-covered table or eaten by candlelight. The coupe glasses, parfait dishes, stemware, and ramekins in which we serve them elevate them to the status of highbrow. And don't forget the bourbon. Its sturdy sophistication doesn't do these desserts a whit of harm.

Old-Fashioned Baked Rice Pudding with Bourbon-Soaked Apricots

My mother talked about loving rice pudding, but strangely she never made it for us. When I was about eight years old, we were visiting my Aunt Donna in Florida, and my mom's mother, Grandma Stella, was staying there for a month. My grandmother made the dish on request from my mom. It was custardy, rich, toothsome, and sweet. I was in heaven. I think my mother never attempted it because she wanted all rice pudding to be her own mom's.

Rice pudding is one of the simplest, most satisfying desserts you can make, and you can do it in less than half an hour. Since it's a blank slate upon which one can impose personal kitchen creativity, I concocted this version, made with oaky-sweet bourbon and deep syrupy apricots.

Makes about 6 individual desserts

Butter, for greasing pan
½ cup dried apricots, chopped
½ cup bourbon
¾ cup short-grain rice
4 cups light cream
1 vanilla bean, split lengthwise and scraped
½ teaspoon freshly grated lemon zest
½ cup sugar
4 egg yolks

Preheat the oven to 300 degrees F. Butter 6 heat-proof 6- to 8-ounce ramekins or custard cups. Place a 9 x 13-inch glass baking dish on a heavy metal baking sheet. (This will become the water bath for the ramekins.)

In a small bowl, cover the apricots with the bourbon, cover loosely with a dishtowel, and set aside.

In a tightly lidded medium-sized heavy saucepan over medium-high heat, bring the rice, cream, vanilla seeds and scrapings, and lemon zest to a simmer. (Reserve the vanilla bean pod and use in making vanilla sugar; see page 99.)

Immediately reduce the heat to the lowest setting possible, cover tightly, and cook for 20 minutes. Turn off the heat, and let the mixture rest for 5 minutes before lifting the lid.

Add the sugar, and stir well. Put the egg yolks in a small, heat-proof bowl or Pyrex measuring cup. Ladle in about half a cup of the hot rice mixture, and stir to temper. Gradually add the tempered egg yolk mixture to the rice mixture, stirring well after each addition.

Spoon the rice pudding into the ramekins, and set them in the glass baking dish. Fill the baking dish two-thirds of the way up the sides of the ramekins with hot water.

Carefully slide the baking sheet holding the water bath into the oven, and bake for 20 minutes, or until golden brown on the top.

Remove from the oven and let the glass baking dish cool on a wire rack. Once cooled, remove the ramekins from the water bath, place on a dishtowel, and divide the bourbon-apricot topping among the puddings.

Store in the refrigerator, tightly covered with plastic wrap or foil, for up to 3 days.

Kentucky Plus

- Try dried plums instead of apricots for a deeper flavor and more old-fashioned feel.
- Skip the topping, and stir in ¼ cup bourbon and 1 cup raisins to the pot with the rice for a bourbony, comforting baked pudding.

Bourbon Panna Cotta

Italian for "cooked cream," panna cotta is reminiscent of flan. Simple and light, it gets some support from gelatin, and slides down the throat like silk.

Most traditionally flavored only with vanilla, panna cotta is ripe for revision. Here's my twist on it, with the flavor of bourbon taking center stage.

Makes 4 individual desserts

2 cups heavy cream
¼ cup granulated sugar
1 vanilla bean, split lengthwise and scraped (see page 99)
3 tablespoons bourbon
1½ tablespoons powdered, unflavored gelatin
½ pint raspberries, for garnish
1 sprig mint, cut into pieces, for garnish

In a small, heavy-bottomed saucepan over medium heat, bring the cream and sugar to a boil, add the seeds and scrapings of the vanilla bean; then immediately reduce the heat and simmer, covered, stirring frequently, for about 10 minutes or until it thickens, coating the back of a spoon.

Put the bourbon in a small bowl, gradually sprinkle in the gelatin, and let stand for 3 minutes.

Remove the cream mixture from the heat, then add the bourbon mixture and stir lightly.

Distribute the mixture evenly among 4 heat-proof glasses, coffee mugs, or ramekins.

Cool to room temperature, then garnish the top of each dessert with a handful of raspberries and a sprig of the mint. Refrigerate for at least 4 hours, then serve chilled.

Store in the refrigerator for up to 3 days, covered tightly with aluminum foil or plastic wrap.

Cinnamon-Bourbon Tiramisu Cups

Dark chocolate, creamy cheese, rich espresso, and the smoke of bourbon make this southern version of Italian tiramisu special. I lean toward this dessert instead of a birthday cake.

In general, I like to make all of the elements of my recipes from scratch. That said, I've been known to tear up an Entenmann's cake for a trifle, or use instant pudding to top stewed fruit. Ladyfingers are made from a tricky dough, and the piping process strikes me as time-consuming and laborious. Since the ladyfingers in this recipe are just a layering vehicle, it's not worth it for me to make them from scratch.

This recipe uses raw eggs, following the traditional way of making tiramisu. If you have concerns, be sure to use very fresh eggs. (See "Raw Eggs—Safe or Not?" on page 94.)

Makes 6 individual desserts

½ cup brewed espresso, at room temperature
3 tablespoons bourbon
2 large eggs, at room temperature, separated
Pinch of salt
½ cup granulated sugar, divided
1 cup mascarpone cheese
12 ladyfingers
1 ounce dark chocolate (70% cacao)
Unsweetened cocoa powder, for garnish

Chill six 6- to 8-ounce dessert cups or ramekins in the refrigerator.

In a medium-sized bowl, mix together the espresso and bourbon. Set it aside.

In a large mixing bowl, using an electric mixer set on medium-high speed, beat the egg whites until they form soft peaks, about 3 minutes. Add half of the sugar and beat until stiff, about 2 minutes. Scrape the egg whites into a small bowl.

In the original bowl, beat the egg yolks with the remaining sugar and the salt until stiff and light-colored, about three minutes. Using a rubber spatula, fold in the mascarpone and stir until smooth.

Fold in half of the beaten egg whites; then fold in the remaining half and combine just until fully incorporated.

Spoon the mascarpone cream into the bottoms of the dessert cups or ramekins, about ½ inch deep.

Drop the ladyfingers, one by one, into the espresso mixture for 10 to 15 seconds until saturated. Break the cookies in half and submerge again, making sure that they have soaked up as much liquid as possible. Layer over the cream in the ramekins, using two full cookies each.

Grate the chocolate over the top of each cup.

Divide the remaining cream among the ramekins, cover them with plastic or aluminum foil, and refrigerate for at least six hours.

Just before serving, dust with cocoa powder.

Store in the refrigerator, tightly covered with plastic wrap or foil, for up to 3 days.

❧ Raw Eggs—Safe or Not?

It's been said that raw egg yolks taste like vanilla and that eating them gives you a health boost. But studies have shown that some raw eggs could carry the salmonella bacteria. In most cases, this bacteria resides only on the shell, so some people, like myself, are comfortable with merely washing the eggs or scalding them in boiling water for 5 seconds before cracking them to release the interior, edible portion.

As there's no sure way to fully ensure that the eggs you use are 100 percent safe, it's up to you to decide what's right for yourself and your family. I recommend not eating raw eggs if you're part of a group at high risk for infections, such as pregnant women or people with compromised immune systems. I'll just say that I eat them regularly in egg shakes, holiday eggnog, on steak tartare, and in salad dressing. My kids are strong and healthy, so I feed them to my whole family. I have an excellent source for fresh eggs and always use wise kitchen hygiene. Within these parameters, most people are fine. Still, if your gut tells you not to eat raw eggs, listen. Consult a doctor if you feel that raw eggs could be the wrong choice for your household. And here's my final thought: These days, I always discuss food allergies and restrictions with those who'll sit at my table. I advise using common sense regarding guests: never serve foods containing raw eggs without full disclosure.

Burnt Sugar and Bourbon Pudding

There's not a thing in the world wrong with a cornstarch-thickened pudding, but luxurious custards using egg yolks as the setting agent are as smooth and rich as it gets. The addition of "burnt" sugar flavor is what makes this custard a standout. The technique of making burnt sugar is similar to caramelizing: you're changing the chemical composition of the sugar by raising it to a high temperature. This process changes the sugar's color to a satisfying deep brown and adds a nutty depth to the taste.

With its glossy and silken texture and layers of rich flavors, all this pudding needs is a tipsy component. It's got it in spades with warm, flavorful bourbon.

Makes 4 individual desserts

2 cups heavy cream
½ vanilla bean, split lengthwise and scraped
½ cup granulated sugar, divided
2 tablespoons bourbon
3 large egg yolks, room temperature
¼ teaspoon salt
Fleur de sel or kosher salt, for sprinkling

Preheat the oven to 300 degrees F.

Combine the cream, the vanilla bean pod, and its seeds and scrapings in a small, heavy-bottomed saucepan set over low heat.

In a separate, medium-sized, heavy-bottomed saucepan set over medium heat, combine 6 tablespoons of sugar and the bourbon, and cook, stirring constantly, until the sugar dissolves. Raise the heat to high and bring the liquid to a boil. Allow it to cook, keeping close watch so that it doesn't burn or bubble over, stirring constantly and scraping down the sides with a heat-proof silicone spatula until the mixture reduces to a light brown syrup, about 3 or 4 minutes.

Using a slotted spoon, remove the vanilla bean pod from the cream and transfer it to a paper towel. (Later, rinse it under cold water and allow it to dry. Reserve the vanilla bean pod to use in making vanilla sugar; see page 99.)

Pour the cream into the bourbon syrup, and bring the mixture to a boil over medium heat stirring occasionally. Once it comes to a boil (this happens quickly!), remove the pan from the heat, and allow it to cool for 20 minutes.

In a medium-sized bowl, whisk together the egg yolks, the remaining sugar, and the salt. Add about half a cup of the warm cream mixture to the egg yolk mixture, and whisk. Add this back to the cream, whisking constantly. Gradually add the rest, and whisk until combined.

Place a 9 x 13-inch glass baking dish on a heavy baking sheet, and set aside.

Using a fine-mesh wire strainer, strain the mixture into a pitcher or large Pyrex measuring cup and divide it among 4 heat-proof 6- to 8-ounce ramekins or custard cups. Sprinkle the top of each with the coarse-grained salt.

Set the ramekins in the baking dish, and fill the dish halfway up the sides of the ramekins with hot water. Bake for an hour, or until set.

Remove from the oven, set the baking dish to a wire rack, and let cool. Once cooled, transfer the ramekins to the refrigerator, and chill for at least 6 hours before serving.

Store in the refrigerator, tightly covered with plastic wrap or foil, for up to 5 days.

❧ *Bourbon Fact*

Drink your bourbon, and eat your greens.

Kentucky's limestone foundation naturally filters iron from its spring water, making the water perfect for bourbon making; iron would ruin the color and taint the flavor of the beverage. To be on the safe side, have a side of spinach with your shot.

Southern-Style Hot Milk Posset

Thickened sweet milk, with liquor thrown in as a sleep aid? Yes, please! This history-rich drink used to be a bit thinner, and was fortified with wine. Given to children and adults alike, it calmed the nerves and beckoned the sandman.

This version, updated with bourbon, is more of a simple, drinkable custard. It's not quite as rich as eggnog, and that's a good quality in a bedtime warmer. Posset, with its ancient roots, has made a comeback with a very modern spin. Since learning about it, my husband and I have happily welcomed it into our winter wind-down routine, along with snuggling on the sofa, wrapping ourselves in my grandmother's crocheted afghans, and fighting our two dogs for legroom.

Makes 4 individual desserts

2 cups heavy cream
⅓ cup granulated sugar
⅛ teaspoon salt
5 tablespoons lemon juice
1 tablespoon bourbon
1 tablespoon honey

In a small, heavy-bottomed saucepan set over medium heat, bring the cream, sugar, and salt to a simmer. (Never bring the posset to a vigorous boil as it will cause the cream to curdle.) Continue simmering for 5 minutes, stirring constantly.

Remove pan from heat and let it cool for 30 minutes.

Strain the cream through a fine-mesh wire strainer into a pitcher or large Pyrex measuring cup, then return the mixture to the pan and stir in the lemon juice and bourbon.

Bring it back to a simmer and cook for 5 more minutes, stirring constantly. Remove it from the heat, and stir in the honey.

Pour even amounts into 4 heat-proof 6- to 8-ounce custard cups or ramekins, and allow to cool on the countertop for 15 minutes.

Once cooled, transfer the ramekins to the refrigerator and chill for at least 6 hours before serving.

Store in the refrigerator, tightly covered with plastic or foil, for up to 5 days.

Kentucky Plus

> For a morning posset, substitute orange juice for lemon juice in equal parts, and leave out the honey.

> For a whiskey sour posset, substitute lime juice for the lemon and agave nectar for the honey, and add a splash of maraschino cherry juice.

My Two Cents about Real Vanilla

Chocolate steals the limelight as the flavor that turns grown women weak and tames tough men into pussycats. I've never understood the second-banana status of vanilla, though. Some people view vanilla as a flavor void, as if vanilla ice cream or yogurt or pudding equates with "plain." I object! Excellent vanilla beans or extract offers a multilayered flavor that's impossible to compare with any other. Earthy, nutty, fruity, spicy, and rich, pure vanilla is in a class by itself.

High-quality vanilla beans are redolent of tropical aromas known only in the fertile rain forests of places like Costa Rica, Tahiti, or Hawaii, the best-known homes of the aromatic flavoring.

There's no denying that a bottle of good-quality vanilla extract has its time and place, but it's not in the same league as a fragrant, oily bean.

Keeping vanilla sugar on hand is the brilliant trade secret of successful home cooks. Simple to make, the labor and cost of concocting this top-shelf ingredient are well worth the labor and cost of concocting it.

Homemade vanilla sugar sits on the shelf beautifully for ages, is very easy to put together, and can be made with the bean pods left over from other recipes. Substitute it spoon to spoon for granulated sugar, and bask in the effect its presence has on your guests.

BUY THE BEST BEAN

The price of a single vanilla bean might turn your hair white, but remember this: one singular bean imparts a huge amount of fragrance and taste, so the cost per use winds up being quite economical.

I suggest buying beans at specialty stores and gourmet kitchen suppliers, because constant turnover ensures that you'll get fresh beans. Only buy beans that have a pungent aroma and an oily sheen on the outside portion of the pod. Inspect the beans for off-odors or mildew. Check packaging for signs of damage or age. Don't pick up the ones with faded labels, water damage, old expiration dates, or broken seals.

VANILLA SUGAR: MADE PURE, WITH LOVE

Put two cups of sugar into a large mixing bowl.

Rinse a vanilla bean under cold water, and cut it in half lengthwise. Using the tip of a sharp knife, open the bean like you would a pole bean. You'll see the sheeny, dark black seeds that look like caviar, and are nearly as precious. Pressing the bean flat against a cutting board, scrape out the seeds with the knife's blade.

Crumble the seeds into the grains of sugar using your fingers. The more pressing you do to release the oils, the more fragrant your sugar will be.

Coarsely chop and place the empty pods into a clean, sterilized jar and cover with the enriched sugar, leaving a half-inch or so of space at the top. Seal and store the jar in a cool, dark place, such as the pantry, larder, or cellar. Every couple of days, roll and shake the sugar to help the vanilla oil mix with the sugar.

After 10 days, start enjoying your vanilla sugar in recipes, stirred into coffee, or sprinkled on oatmeal or cream of wheat.

Spiked Banana Pudding with Bourbonilla Wafers

❧ I think that just about everyone who grew up down South lets out an involuntary "Awww . . ." when banana pudding gets mentioned. Except the speaker usually says "puddin'" if he or she is talking about what we're all remembering: a big bowl layered with sliced bananas, soft and mushy saturated vanilla wafers, and usually whipped cream.

Here's a Kentucky-style version that adds bourbon to two elements: the wafers and the pudding. If you simply can't get enough bourbon, use Bourbon Whipped Cream (page 71) for the topping.

Makes about 4 dozen wafers, about 4 cups pudding, and about 4 cups whipped cream; assemble into 1 large trifle in a 3-quart bowl (serves 12 to 14)

FOR THE PUDDING
1⅓ cups granulated sugar
½ cup cornstarch
½ teaspoon salt
5 cups milk
8 large egg yolks
4 tablespoons (½ stick) butter, chilled
    and cut into pieces
2 teaspoons vanilla extract
1 tablespoon bourbon

FOR THE WAFERS
5 tablespoons butter, softened
1 cup sugar
1 large egg
2 teaspoons pure vanilla extract
2 teaspoons bourbon
¼ cup milk
2 cups all-purpose flour
2 teaspoons baking powder
¼ teaspoon salt

FOR THE WHIPPED CREAM
4 cups heavy cream
2 tablespoons granulated sugar

FOR THE BANANA LAYER
4 large ripe bananas

TO MAKE THE PUDDING
In a medium-sized, heavy-bottomed saucepan, off of the heat, whisk together the sugar, cornstarch, and salt. Very gradually (a few spoonsful at a time) whisk in the milk, making sure to dissolve cornstarch before heating the liquid. (If the cornstarch hasn't dissolved, you'll get lumps, like in poorly made gravy.) Once the mixture is well combined, whisk in the egg yolks.

Cook over medium heat, whisking constantly, until a few large bubbles begin to form and pop. Reduce the heat to low, and continue to cook for about 1 minute, still whisking constantly.

Remove the pan from the heat, and immediately pour the mixture through a fine-mesh wire strainer into a medium-sized bowl. Stir in the butter, vanilla, and bourbon.

Cover the pudding with plastic wrap, pressing it gently onto the surface (to prevent a skin from forming). Chill for at least 4 hours.

TO MAKE THE WAFERS
Preheat the oven to 350 degrees F. Line two 9 x 13-inch baking sheets with parchment and set them aside.

In a large mixing bowl, using an electric mixer set on medium-high speed, cream together the butter and sugar until light and fluffy, about 3 minutes. Add the egg, vanilla, bourbon, and milk, and mix until combined, about 3 minutes.

In a separate, large mixing bowl, whisk together the flour, baking powder, and salt.

A little at a time, add the flour mixture to the butter and sugar mixture, beating after each addition to incorporate. Once a dough is formed, refrigerate to chill the batter in the refrigerator for at least 10 minutes before scooping onto the baking sheets.

Drop the batter by teaspoonsful onto the prepared pans, forming balls with your fingertips. Then, flatten the balls slightly with the heel of your hand.

Bake for 15 minutes, or until brown on top and crispy at the edges. Remove from the oven and set the baking sheets onto wire racks to cool slightly before removing the cookies from the pan and transferring them directly to the racks to cool completely.

TO MAKE THE BOURBON WHIPPED CREAM
(See page 71.) Whip the cream, and set aside in the refrigerator.

TO ASSEMBLE
The idea is to create even layers of wafers, whipped cream, bananas, and pudding.

Slice the bananas into rounds, and set aside. Line the bottom of a 3-quart trifle bowl with the wafers. Spoon a layer of whipped cream about ½ inch thick over the wafers. Layer on sliced bananas. Cover with chilled pudding, and add another layer of wafers. Keep repeating layers of whipped cream, bananas, pudding, and wafers until you've used up all the ingredients or the bowl is full, ending with whipped cream.

Refrigerate for at least 6 hours so the wafers can soften.

Store in the refrigerator, tightly covered with plastic wrap or foil, for up to 5 days.

White Chocolate and Bourbon Crème Brûlée

⟫ The lethal richness of white chocolate blended with the multilayered flavor of bourbon makes for a luxe après-dinner treat. You'll have trouble putting your finger on which part of this smooth delight you like best: the flavors or the thrill of cracking that caramelized shell on top with your dessert spoon.

Makes 6 individual desserts

2 cups heavy cream
6 egg yolks
½ cup plus 6 tablespoons vanilla sugar (page 99), divided (or you can use granulated sugar plus ½ teaspoon pure vanilla extract)
6 ounces white baking chocolate, finely chopped
2 teaspoons bourbon

Place a 9 x 13-inch glass baking dish on a heavy baking sheet, and set aside.

In a medium-sized, heavy-bottomed saucepan over medium heat, bring the cream to a light simmer. Once small bubbles form, reduce the heat to the lowest setting possible.

In a medium-sized mixing bowl, whisk together the egg yolks and ½ cup sugar until the mixture is pale yellow and the sugar is dissolved.

Add a few tablespoons of warm cream to the egg mixture, whisking to combine.

Gradually add the rest of the cream, whisking constantly.

Add the chocolate, bourbon, and vanilla (if using) and whisk until the chocolate has melted and the mixture is smooth. Divide the mixture evenly among 6 heat-proof 6- to 8-ounce custard cups or ramekins.

Set the ramekins in the baking dish, and fill the dish halfway up the sides of the ramekins with hot water. Bake for about 45 minutes, or until set.

Remove from the oven and set the baking dish on a wire rack to cool. Once cooled, transfer the ramekins to the refrigerator, and chill for at least 6 hours.

Before serving, bring to room temperature for 15 minutes, sprinkle the top of each ramekin with 1 tablespoon of vanilla sugar (or granulated sugar), and either caramelize with a small culinary blow torch, if you have one, or by setting the ramekins on a baking sheet and caramelizing under a broiler, watching constantly so they don't burn.

Store in the refrigerator, tightly covered with plastic wrap or foil, for up to 5 days.

Pumpkin Gingerbread Trifle with Bourbon Whipped Cream

Make this stunning trifle, and for the first time in the history of your Thanksgiving table, your roast turkey may take a backseat in the wow factor department.

If you are lucky enough to have fridge space (a cold garage works in a pinch), you can make this a day ahead, and that time-saver only serves to make the flavors more fabulous.

An alternative to your basic pumpkin or apple pie, this giant bourbon-tinted parfait will be the thing your guests leave your table talking about.

Makes 1 9-inch square cake, about 4 cups pudding, and about 4 cups whipped cream; assemble into 1 large trifle in a 3-quart bowl (serves 12 to 14)

FOR THE PUDDING
1⅓ cups granulated sugar
½ cup cornstarch
½ teaspoon salt
5 cups milk
8 large egg yolks
4 tablespoons (½ stick) butter, chilled and cut into pieces
2 teaspoons vanilla extract
1 tablespoon bourbon

FOR THE GINGERBREAD
½ cup (1 stick) butter, plus 1 tablespoon for greasing pan
½ cup granulated sugar
1 large egg
1 cup molasses
2½ cups all-purpose flour, plus more for dusting pan
1½ teaspoons baking soda
1 teaspoon ground cinnamon
1 teaspoon ground ginger
½ teaspoon ground cloves
½ teaspoon salt
1 cup hot water

FOR THE SPICED PUMPKIN PUREE
1 (15-ounce) can packed pumpkin
½ cup light brown sugar, packed
¼ cup pure maple syrup
¼ cup bourbon
1 tablespoon pure vanilla extract
1 tablespoon finely chopped fresh ginger
½ teaspoon ground cinnamon
½ teaspoon ground cardamom

FOR THE WHIPPED CREAM
4 cups heavy cream
2 tablespoons granulated sugar

FOR THE TOPPING

1 cup snickerdoodle crumbs (from 4 to 6 large cookies)

TO MAKE THE PUDDING

In a medium-sized, heavy-bottomed saucepan, off of the heat, whisk together the sugar, cornstarch, and salt. Very gradually (a few spoonsful at a time) whisk in the milk, making sure to dissolve cornstarch before heating the liquid. (If the cornstarch hasn't dissolved, you'll get lumps, like in poorly made gravy.) Once the mixture is well combined, whisk in the egg yolks.

Cook over medium heat, whisking constantly, until a few large bubbles begin to form and pop. Reduce the heat to low, and continue to cook for about 1 minute, still whisking constantly.

Remove the pan from the heat, and immediately pour the mixture through a fine-mesh wire strainer into a medium-sized bowl. Stir in the butter, vanilla, and bourbon.

Cover the pudding with plastic wrap, pressing it gently onto the surface (to prevent a skin from forming). Chill for at least 4 hours.

TO MAKE THE GINGERBREAD

Preheat the oven to 350 degrees F. Butter and flour a 9-inch square pan.

In a large mixing bowl, cream together the butter and sugar until light and fluffy, about 3 minutes. Beat in the egg until incorporated, about 1 minute. Beat in the molasses until blended and smooth, about 1 minute more.

In a separate, large mixing bowl, whisk together the flour, baking soda, cinnamon, ginger, cloves, and salt. A little at a time, add the flour mixture to the creamed mixture, beating well after each addition, about 2 minutes.

Add the hot water, and beat until smooth, about 1 minute.

Pour the batter into the prepared pan.

Bake 1 hour, or until a wooden cake tester or metal skewer inserted into the center comes out clean. Remove from the oven and set the pan on a wire baking rack to cool for 30 minutes.

TO MAKE THE SPICED PUMPKIN PUREE

In a large mixing bowl, combine the pumpkin, brown sugar, maple syrup, bourbon, vanilla, ginger, cinnamon, and cardamom, and fold together with a rubber spatula until smooth and creamy.

TO MAKE THE WHIPPED CREAM

(See page 122.) Whip the cream, and set aside in the refrigerator.

TO MAKE THE TOPPING

Put the cookies in a heavy-duty zip-top freezer bag, and roll them with a rolling pin until coarsely crushed.

TO ASSEMBLE

The idea is to create layers of gingerbread, pudding, puree, and whipped cream, then garnish with the crushed cookies.

Line the bottom of a 3-quart trifle bowl with torn-up cubes of gingerbread.

Spoon on a layer of pudding, followed by a layer of puree, then a layer of whipped cream.

Keep repeating until you've used up all the ingredients or the bowl is full, ending with whipped cream. Garnish with the crushed cookies.

Refrigerate for at least 6 hours so the wafers can soften.

Store in the refrigerator, tightly covered with plastic wrap or foil, for up to 5 days.

❧ *Bourbon Fact*

Small, but mighty.

Before 1920 and the start of Prohibition, there were around 2,000 distilleries in the state of Kentucky. Today, there are around 20.

Butterscotch Pudding with Cinnamon-Bourbon Meringue

⤜ The only flaw I've ever found with this satiny dessert is that I can't figure out what a serving size is. I'm careful to make this only when there's a crowd, because I honestly cannot control myself when it comes to the brown-sugary, buttery flavor and the pungent, candied air that is the cinnamon meringue.

Makes about 8 servings

FOR THE PUDDING
¼ cup (½ stick) butter
¾ cup light brown sugar, packed
3 tablespoons molasses
2¼ cups whole milk, divided
1 cup heavy cream
½ vanilla bean, split lengthwise and scraped
3 large egg yolks
3 tablespoons cornstarch
1 teaspoon pure vanilla extract
¼ teaspoon salt

FOR THE MERINGUE
½ cup light brown sugar, packed
2 tablespoons bourbon
1 teaspoon ground cinnamon
3 large egg whites
¼ teaspoon cream of tartar

TO MAKE THE PUDDING
In a medium-sized, heavy-bottomed saucepan, combine the butter, ¾ cup brown sugar, and the molasses and set it over medium heat. Simmer, stirring constantly, until the sugar dissolves, about 3 to 5 minutes.

In a separate, small, heavy-bottomed saucepan, combine 1¾ cups milk and the cream. Bring to a slow simmer over medium-low heat, then add the vanilla bean pod, seeds, and scrapings. Simmer for about 10 minutes, stirring occasionally, taking care never to bring it to a boil. Using a slotted spoon, remove the vanilla bean pod from the cream, and transfer it to a paper towel. (Later, rinse the pod under cold water and allow it to dry, then use in making vanilla sugar; see page 99.)

Gradually add the milk mixture to the sugar mixture, whisking until combined. Remove from heat.

In a small bowl, whisk together egg yolks, the remaining ½ cup milk, the cornstarch, vanilla, and salt.

Gradually add about ½ cup of the hot warm milk and sugar mixture to the yolk mixture, whisking constantly to temper.

Add the yolk mixture to remaining hot mixture in the saucepan, again whisking constantly. Cook over medium heat, stirring frequently until it thickens, about the consistency of eggnog.

Remove the custard from the heat and pour it into a 1-quart glass baking dish.

Cover the pudding with plastic wrap, pressing it gently onto the top of the pudding (to prevent a skin from forming). Chill for at least 4 hours.

TO MAKE THE MERINGUE

In a medium-sized, heavy-bottomed saucepan, combine ½ cup brown sugar, bourbon, and cinnamon. Simmer over medium-low heat, stirring constantly, about 5 to 8 minutes, until the syrup thickens to the consistency of warm honey and turns a deep reddish-amber color.

Using an electric mixer set on medium-high speed, beat the egg whites and cream of tartar until stiff peaks form, about 3 minutes.

Gradually add the warm sugar syrup, and beat until the mixture is thick and has a high sheen, about 2 to 3 more minutes.

TO ASSEMBLE

Preheat the broiler.

Take the chilled pudding out of the refrigerator, and gently spoon on dollops of the meringue, forming peaks with the back of a spoon.

Set the pudding under the hot broiler, watching constantly until the peaks of the meringue have browned. Once browned, serve immediately.

Store in the refrigerator, tightly covered with plastic wrap or foil, for up to 3 days.

❧ *Bourbon Fact*

During World War II, bourbon distilleries were converted to make fuel alcohol and penicillin. Having scarcely reopened following the repeal of Prohibition, the factories were repurposed to aid the war effort. Both the fuel and penicillin are products of fermentation, so distilleries were the obvious choice to produce the much-needed commodities. Kentucky whiskey lovers sacrificed, and the war was won.

Spicy Chocolate Mousse with a Whiff of Bourbon

⤳ I love the mismatch of the airy, delicate mousse with the sneak-up-on-you kick of the cayenne pepper. The smoothness of the bourbon and the cool temperature will soothe any temporarily angry taste buds, and you'll be reaching for your spoon to experience the thrill of the next bite.

Makes 4 individual desserts

1 cup heavy cream
¼ cup confectioners' sugar
¼ cup bourbon
Pinch ground cayenne pepper
Scant pinch finely ground black pepper
6 ounces dark chocolate (Valrhona Le Noir
    Extra Amer 85% Cacao, if you can find it,
    but at least 70% cacao), chopped
4 large egg whites
½ teaspoon salt

Chill four 6- to 8-ounce dessert cups or coupe glasses in the refrigerator.

In a medium-sized, heavy-bottomed saucepan over medium-high heat, bring the heavy cream and sugar to a boil; then remove the pan from the heat.

Stir in the bourbon and the two peppers.

Add the chocolate, and let it rest for 5 minutes without stirring.

Whisk the chocolate cream mixture until it's smooth, and gently scoop it into a large bowl using a rubber spatula.

In a separate, medium-sized mixing bowl, beat together the egg whites and the salt using an electric mixer set on high speed until they form stiff peaks.

Using a rubber spatula, fold about one-quarter of the beaten whites into the chocolate mixture to lighten it. Then gently fold in the rest, working the mousse as little as possible in order not to collapse it.

Divide the mousse into the chilled cups or glasses, and chill for at least 4 hours before serving.

Store in the refrigerator in individual dishes covered tightly with plastic wrap or foil for up to 3 days.

Old-Fashioned Bourbon and Milk Pudding

⤳ Bourbon and milk. It's what lulled many a Kentucky infant to sleep in days gone by. Eat a lovely bowl of this, and you'll see why. My advice? Be in your pajamas and near a soft couch.

Makes 4 individual desserts

½ cup dark brown sugar, packed

3 tablespoons water

1½ cups whole milk

½ cup heavy cream

¼ cup cornstarch

¼ teaspoon salt

¼ teaspoon nutmeg

3 tablespoons vanilla sugar (page 99), or use granulated sugar plus ½ teaspoon pure vanilla extract

3 large egg yolks

¼ cup half-and-half

1 tablespoon butter, cold and cut into pieces

4 tablespoons bourbon

Chill six 6- to 8-ounce heat-proof custard cups or ramekins in the refrigerator.

Combine the brown sugar and water in a medium-sized saucepan set over medium-high heat, and bring the mixture to a simmer, stirring occasionally. Simmer until the sugar dissolves and a syrup forms, about 3 to 5 minutes.

Stir in the milk and cream and bring to a simmer, stirring occasionally. Reduce the heat to low, and let it simmer on very low heat while you prepare the other mixtures. Stir occasionally, and take care never to bring it to a boil.

In a medium-sized mixing bowl, whisk together the cornstarch, salt, and nutmeg, and set aside.

In a large, heat-proof mixing bowl, combine the vanilla sugar (or granulated sugar plus vanilla extract) and egg yolks, and beat together using an electric mixer set on medium speed, about 2 minutes. Add the half-and-half, and the cornstarch mixture, then beat again until combined, about 3 minutes

Working in thirds, add the warm milk mixture to the sugar, half-and-half, and cornstarch mixture, beating for about 30 seconds after each addition. Once blended, return the mixture to the pan, and bring it to a simmer over medium-high heat, whisking constantly.

Once the first large bubble breaks on the surface, reduce the heat to medium-low, and cook, whisking occasionally, until the pudding thickens to the consistency of heavy eggnog, about 5 to 10 minutes.

Remove the pan from the heat and add the butter, vanilla (if using), and bourbon, and beat with the electric mixer set on low speed until combined, about 1 minute.

Pour the pudding into the serving dishes, and chill for at least 6 hours.

Store in the refrigerator, covered tightly with foil or plastic wrap, for up to 3 days.

Dark Chocolate Bread Pudding with Lemon-Bourbon Sauce

Bread pudding was at one time thought of as peasant food, a way to use up the leftover stale loaves in order to economize. Fair enough. Food is food. But add bourbon and dark chocolate, and the bread is transformed into a pastry. Top it with gooey, sticky lemon sauce with its bright contrasting tang, and that old loaf of bread will go out having had its day in the sun.

Makes 15 servings

FOR THE PUDDING
1 tablespoon butter, for greasing pan
1 large loaf French bread, cubed (about 1 pound, or 6 cups)
4 cups milk
3 large eggs
2 cups granulated sugar
2 tablespoons pure vanilla extract
¼ teaspoon nutmeg
¼ teaspoon ground cinnamon
¼ teaspoon allspice
1 cup bittersweet chocolate chips

FOR THE SAUCE
1 large egg, plus 1 egg yolk
½ cup (1 stick) butter
1 cup sugar
1 large egg, plus one egg yolk
3 tablespoons lemon juice
2 tablespoons bourbon

TO MAKE THE PUDDING
Preheat oven to 350 degrees F. Butter a 9 x 13-inch glass baking dish.

In a large mixing bowl, combine the bread and milk, stir with a large spoon to wet the bread, and set aside.

In a separate large mixing bowl, whisk together eggs, sugar, vanilla, nutmeg, cinnamon, and allspice until smooth, about 3 minutes. Stir in the chocolate chips.

Pour the egg–chocolate chip mixture into the bowl with the soaking bread. Set it aside on the countertop, loosely covered with a dishtowel, for one hour, stirring occasionally to moisten and combine.

Pour the bread pudding mixture into the prepared baking dish.

Bake for 45 minutes, or until crispy at the edges and set in the center. Remove from the oven and cool on a wire rack for at least 20 minutes before cutting and serving topped with the Lemon-Bourbon Sauce.

Store in the refrigerator, tightly covered with plastic wrap or foil, for up to 3 days.

TO MAKE THE LEMON-BOURBON SAUCE
In a small bowl, whisk together the egg and egg yolk until light and fluffy, about 4 minutes.

In a medium-sized saucepan set over low heat, combine the butter and sugar, whisking constantly until the sugar has melted, making sure it doesn't burn. Once the sugar has melted, pour the mixture into a blender.

Add about a tablespoon of the egg mixture, and blend on medium-low speed, for about 45 seconds. A little at a time, add more egg, blending for 45 seconds each time. Don't do it all at once or the egg will cook and set!

Once smooth, add the lemon juice, and blend for 1 minute. Add the bourbon, and blend for 1 minute more. Pour the sauce over the pudding, and serve.

Store the sauce and the pudding in the refrigerator in separate, tightly lidded containers for up to 5 days.

Apple-Bourbon Syllabub

The syllabub is a popular eighteenth-century dessert, made by chemically changing cream with acid, usually lemon juice, and mixing it with wine. Once mixed and allowed to settle, syllabubs separate into a two-part mixture wherein the cream rises to the top, and the nondairy liquids sink to the bottom. The oldest syllabubs were made by milking a cow directly into a bucket of wine. Back then, dairy desserts were generally served warm (think of the cow's body temperature) or at room temperature. Today, we serve syllabubs, as we do most dairy desserts, chilled.

Ultra-light, with the finish of citrus and alcohol, syllabubs make a great palate cleanser.

The syllabub offered here would be considered a solid syllabub, more substantial than some of the blends in days of yore. It also gains gravitas from the bourbon.

Makes 8 individual desserts

2 cups heavy cream
1 cup apple cider
2 tablespoons lemon juice
2 tablespoons bourbon
2 tablespoons sugar

Place a large jar (at least 2 quarts and up to a gallon in volume), along with 8 coupe or martini glasses, in the refrigerator and chill for at least an hour.

Combine all of the ingredients in the jar, and screw the lid on firmly.

Shake the jar briskly for at least 5 minutes. You should begin to feel the resistance of the liquid lessen as it turns into frothy, substantial cream. If you feel or see that the liquid has not whipped into a thickened, creamy mousse, keep shaking for at least 3 minutes, and up to 10.

Remove the lid from the jar, and use a rubber spatula to gently scoop the dessert out of the jar and into the chilled dessert glasses, and let them sit until separated. Serve at room temperature or chilled.

Bourbon-and-Ginger Pumpkin Mousse

⟩ The spicy heat of ginger blended with the warming heat of bourbon is the perfect counterpoint to the earthy, sweet taste of pumpkin. Lightened with air, this mousse is almost just a suggestion of a dessert. Almost. Fluffy as it is, the eggs give this dessert substance. You'll walk away from the table knowing you've experienced something. Something good!

Makes 4 individual desserts

½ cup granulated sugar
¼ cup pure maple syrup
¼ cup bourbon
½ teaspoon salt
1 teaspoon minced fresh ginger
1 teaspoon ground cinnamon
¼ teaspoon ground nutmeg
¼ teaspoon ground cloves
8 large eggs, separated
1 (15-ounce) can packed pumpkin
2 tablespoons finely chopped candied ginger,
    for garnish

Fill a medium-sized saucepan about one-fourth full with water, and set it over medium heat. Place a medium-sized metal bowl over the pan (you're creating a double boiler), and add the sugar, maple syrup, bourbon, salt, fresh ginger, cinnamon, nutmeg, cloves, and egg yolks. Stir the mixture to combine, then cook it, whisking until large bubbles form, and until thickened and pale, about 8 minutes. Remove from the heat, and set aside.

In medium-sized mixing bowl, whisk the egg whites until stiff peaks form. Add the canned pumpkin, and fold it in using a rubber spatula.

Add the pumpkin mixture to the warm bourbon mixture, and fold together until smooth and uniform.

Divide the mousse among four 6- to 8-ounce dessert glasses and sprinkle on the candied ginger, dividing evenly.

Store in the refrigerator, tightly covered with plastic or foil, for up to 2 days.

Light Chocolate Layer Cake with
Bourbon and Cream Cheese Frosting

Always-in-the-Pantry
Bourbon Pound Cake

Bourbony Butter Kuchen

Lane Cake

Nutty Bourbon Fudge
No-Crust Pie

Grandma Rose's Big Race Pie

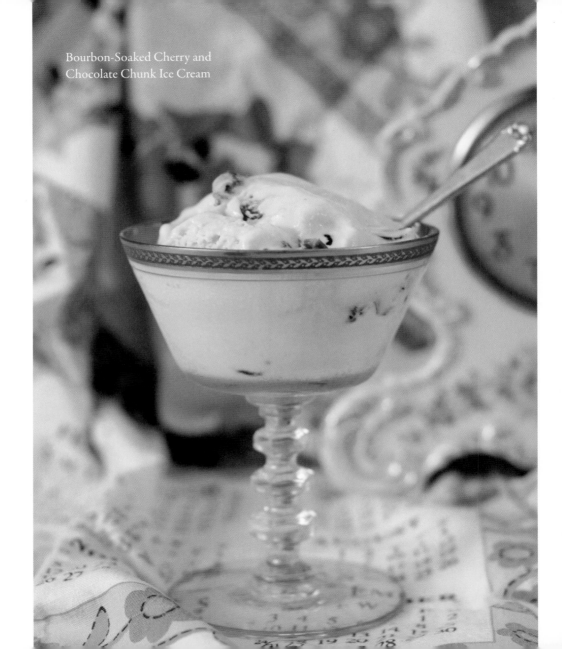

Bourbon-Soaked Cherry and
Chocolate Chunk Ice Cream

Microwave Bourbon-Pecan Fudge

Bourbon-Sugared Pecans

Sweet and Boozy Graham
Cracker Candies

Simple Microwave Peanut Brittle
with Bourbon

Bourbon-Buttermilk Syrup

Traditional Orange Marmalade
with Bourbon

Strawberry Bourbon
Milkshake with White
Chocolate Mint Mousse

Bourbon and Honey
Egg Cream

Bourbon and Maple Pots de Crème

The name *pots de crème* teases my mind toward French cuisine. That's not out of line, given the French fingerprints all over Kentucky's origins. The very name "Bourbon" refers to the dynasty of French rulers in place when bourbon was invented. With the addition of pure maple syrup and real bourbon, there's no denying that this haute cuisine custard is a true American original.

Makes 8 individual desserts

2 tablespoons granulated sugar
¾ teaspoon salt
2 large eggs, plus 3 large egg yolks
2 tablespoons bourbon
1 teaspoon pure vanilla extract
1½ cups whole milk
1½ cups heavy cream
⅓ cup pure maple syrup
Whipped cream, for garnish
Bourbon-Sugared Pecans, for garnish (page 157)

Preheat the oven to 350 degrees F. Place a 9 x 13-inch glass baking dish on a heavy metal baking sheet. (This will become the water bath for the ramekins.)

Combine the sugar, salt, eggs, egg yolks, bourbon, and vanilla in a medium-sized mixing bowl, and whisk until smooth.

Add the milk, cream, and maple syrup, and whisk until smooth. Pour the mixture into a large glass measuring cup, and divide it evenly among eight 6- to 8-ounce custard cups or ramekins.

Set the ramekins into the baking dish and fill it with hot water halfway up the sides.

Bake for an hour, or until set.

Remove from the oven and place the baking dish on a wire rack to cool. Once cooled, transfer the ramekins to the refrigerator, and chill for at least 6 hours before serving. To serve, garnish by adding a dollop of whipped cream to each ramekin, then dotting with Bourbon-Sugared Pecans.

Store in the refrigerator, tightly covered with plastic wrap or foil, for up to 5 days.

5 Frozen Delights

❧ There must have been a glitch on history's timeline when ice cream became the domain of children. Barring the wares of wildly pricey artisanal ice-cream stores, it's widely accepted that ice cream is kid stuff.

Dig deep and you'll find that wasn't always so. Certainly in the days before air conditioning, adults found heading to the local ice cream parlor to be a respectable way to pass an evening. And don't forget: soda fountains turned into small towns' social hubs during the Prohibition years in America. This was mainly due to the fact that soda jerks and pharmacists shared the same digs, and booze could be gotten with a prescription. Still, that's where you'd find the men of the community gathered round, unabashedly digging into sundaes and licking cones.

My grandparents were of this generation and either didn't know to—or didn't bother to—hide their adoration of the stuff. Their preferred flavors were maple nut, butter pecan, and orange sherbet. There was a time when I would have called these "old people flavors," myself preferring candy-packed, fudge-rippled, and chocolate types.

As I aged, my palate saw the light. I haven't lost my love of chocolate, but I understand now why those other tastes beckon. Here are some treats made all the more appealing with the addition of bourbon.

Watermelon Julep Pops

➤ Cool watermelon, fresh mint, and slushy bourbon. These freezer treats are a Kentucky summer on a stick. I remember being in the country, buying watermelons off the backs of farmers' trucks for mere pennies a pound during the height of the season. And it seems every Louisville backyard has at least a corner that's been overtaken by prolific and insistent mint stems. Picnics featuring creative fare made from these ingredients were as normal as rain when I was a child. I can almost smell the sweetness of the watermelon and the sharpness of the mint, usually floating on the fragrance of bourbon. If you don't have a picnic planned and you can't make it to the track to get your julep fix, these pops should salve the wound.

When it comes to frozen desserts, the more alcohol that's involved, the longer the freeze time needed. I wanted the bourbon to stand out in these pops, so make sure to allow at least one day, if not longer, for them to freeze hard.

Makes about 8 pops, depending on your molds

6 cups seeded watermelon chunks (from about one 4-pound watermelon)
¼ cup granulated sugar
2 tablespoons fresh-squeezed lemon juice (from 1 small lemon)
¼ cup bourbon
⅛ teaspoon salt
2 tablespoons chopped fresh mint

In a blender, combine the watermelon, sugar, lemon juice, bourbon, and salt. Blend on high until you have a smooth, uniform texture, about 3 minutes.

Pour the mixture through a fine-mesh wire strainer, reserving the liquid and discarding the solids. (Press down with your hands to get as much liquid as possible.)

Pour the liquid into the molds and freeze without inserting the sticks or handles. After 30 minutes to an hour, or at the point at which the pops are half-frozen and still the consistency of a melty sorbet, stir a pinch of the mint into each mold, and distribute it evenly using a skewer or a chopstick.

Slide the pops back into the freezer and freeze for another 30 minutes, or until pops are firm enough to hold the stick or handle upright, and insert it.

Freeze for 24 hours, or until the pops are solid and will hold up firmly on the sticks or handles.

Store in the freezer for up to 2 weeks, covered or in a zip-top bag to help stave off freezer burn or off flavors.

Bourbon-Soaked Cherry and Chocolate Chunk Ice Cream

⤳ As if chocolate and cherries weren't a heady enough combination, along comes bourbon to join the fun and truly make you swoon!

I'm not sure what's the most fun about this delicious dessert: eating it or drinking the cherry-infused bourbon that's left over.

Makes 1 quart

¼ cup dried cherries
¾ cup bourbon, for soaking cherries
2 cups half-and-half
1 cup heavy cream
1 cup vanilla sugar (see page 99), or use granulated
    sugar plus ½ teaspoon pure
    vanilla extract
½ teaspoon salt
½ cup dark chocolate chunks (I like Ghirardelli)

At least 1 day, and up to 2 weeks in advance, combine the dried cherries and the bourbon in a tightly lidded jar. Shake the jar briskly from time to time to infuse.

When it's time to make the ice cream, combine the half-and-half, cream, vanilla sugar (or granulated sugar plus vanilla extract), and salt in a large saucepan set over medium-high heat.

Kentucky Plus

⤳ If you don't have dried cherries, raisins work deliciously.

⤳ For a subtler, more velvety ice cream, use white chocolate chunks.

⤳ If you like a more textured ice cream that satisfies like a meal, add ¾ cup toasted almonds.

Affix a clip-on candy or frying thermometer to the side of the pan. Keeping close watch and stirring constantly, bring the mixture to 170 degrees F. Remove from heat.

Drain the dried cherries, reserving the liquid to sip straight or use in cocktails.

Allow the milk mixture to cool for 15 minutes, then stir in soaked cherries. Stir to combine, transfer the mixture to a tightly lidded container, and chill overnight in the refrigerator.

The next day, stir in the chocolate chunks. Freeze the mixture in an ice cream maker according to the manufacturer's instructions. Because of the alcohol, the ice cream will not freeze hard in the machine, but it will become aerated, and the texture will change to that of a semifreddo.

Transfer the mixture back to the tightly lidded container, and freeze for at least 4 hours before serving.

Store in the freezer, in the same lidded container, for up to 2 weeks.

Spiked Sweet Tea Granitas

These granitas begin life as a spoonable dessert. But let your attention drift, and before you know it, you'll have a slushy cocktail on your hands. These are the kinds of choices I like. Do I eat it fast, or let it melt? It's a win-win.

Makes 4 individual desserts

4 cups water, divided
3 black tea bags
⅔ cup plus 2 teaspoons granulated sugar, divided
¼ cup heavy cream
Whipped cream, for topping (see page 122)
4 strips lemon zest, for garnish
4 sprigs mint, for garnish
½ to 1 cup bourbon

In a small saucepan set over high heat, bring 3 cups of water to a brisk simmer. Turn off the heat, add the tea bags, then cover and steep for 10 minutes.

In a medium-sized, heat-proof bowl, whisk ⅔ cup of the sugar vigorously into 1 cup of cool water until it dissolves, about 3 minutes. Set it aside.

After 10 minutes, remove the tea bags from the saucepan, squeezing them gently into the pan before discarding them, then pour the warm tea into the sugar-water mixture, and stir to combine.

Pour the sweetened tea into an 8 x 8-inch square baking dish, and put it in the freezer. Freeze for 1 hour, then scrape the slush with a fork to break up the ice crystals. Return the pan to the freezer for another hour or two, or until it freezes almost solid.

Meanwhile, combine the heavy cream and the remaining 2 teaspoons sugar. Beat them together using an electric mixer set on medium-high speed until light and fluffy and soft peaks form, about 5 minutes.

To serve, scrape the granita with a fork, and divide the mixture evenly among 4 dessert glasses or martini glasses. Top each with a dollop of whipped cream, a twist of lemon zest, and a sprig of mint. In front of each guest, pour 1 to 2 ounces of bourbon around the inside of the glass, avoiding the garnish, so that it pools in the bottom. Serve immediately to ensure spoonability.

Store the granita in the freezer, in its pan, tightly covered with plastic or foil, for up to 1 week. Store the whipped cream in the refrigerator in a tightly covered lidded container for 1 day.

Why Buy Tubs and Cans? The Secrets to Perfect Whipped Cream

Real whipped cream is worth the trouble. Period. It's fluffy and creamy and adds texture and richness when dolloped onto pies, custards, warmed fruit, and puddings. Making homemade whipped cream isn't rocket science, but knowing these few tricks will ensure excellent results, every time.

- *Always begin with cold, heavy cream*. Chilled, heavy cream whips up with the most ease and the airiest results.
- *Use a very large mixing bowl*. You want to make sure there's lots of space in which to whip air into the cream without sloshes and spatters. If possible, plan ahead and chill the mixing bowl and your beaters or whisk for 15 minutes or longer before starting. Metal is the best choice for the bowl itself and all the accompanying utensils. One cup of heavy cream yields about 4 cups of whipped cream, when whipped properly.
- *Take it slow, to start*. Whipping or beating slowly at the beginning will reduce spilling and splattering.
- *Add sugar or flavoring liquids, such as vanilla or bourbon, once the cream starts to thicken*. Get the party started first, then the whipped cream will have the heft to support the other ingredients.
- *Increase your mixer's speed (or your elbow grease) if you add sugar or liquid flavorings*. Whip, beat, or whisk the cold cream until soft peaks are formed. To test for soft peaks, lift a beater or whisk from bowl and observe. A soft peak should appear. It should be strong enough to hold its shape and not droop sideways, but not look stiff like meringue.
- *Stop while you're ahead*. Perfectly whipped cream dollops nicely and holds a smooth, creamy texture. If you beat cream past the point of perfection, into stiff peaks, the texture will become grainy and will turn into butter.

Whipped cream is best served freshly whipped, but it doesn't suffer too much from sitting in the fridge, tightly covered. I make mine ahead of time at Thanksgiving, so there's one fewer project going in the kitchen at the last minute. My southern neighbor swears by using confectioners' sugar to simultaneously sweeten and stabilize whipped cream when she makes it in advance or plans for it to last more than a day. In our house, whipped cream rarely makes it through the night, but a few spoonsful of the sweet, powdery stuff won't hurt a thing.

Coconut Semifreddo with Bourbon Ball Chunks

⌁ Semifreddo is a luscious frozen dessert from the distant branches of the ice cream family tree. Happily, it's just as delicious as traditional ice cream in its own unique way, and it's quicker and simpler to make.

As with any alcoholic dessert, this one requires patience and time to harden. Don't forget, though, semifreddo means "half-cold," which translates to "half-frozen," so no matter how long you wait, it'll never firm up like real ice cream. Is that a bad thing? Not at all. Enjoy it for what it is.

Makes about 8 servings

1 (13.5 ounce) can unsweetened coconut milk
1 (14 ounce) can sweetened condensed milk
Zest of 1 small lemon
¼ teaspoon kosher salt
1½ heavy cream, cold
1 cup chopped, frozen bourbon balls (from about
　6 to 8 candies; for Betty Lou's Bourbon Balls,
　see page 144)

Kentucky Plus

⌁ For a semifreddo that mimics a nougat, substitute chopped Vanilla-Bourbon Marshmallows (page 153) for the bourbon balls, and add one cup toasted whole almonds.

⌁ For a smooth, tropical, and boozy semifreddo, skip the bourbon balls, and add 3 tablespoons Toasted Almond and Bourbon Syrup for Cocoa (page 139) when you fold in the whipped cream.

Line a 4½ x 8½-inch loaf pan with parchment, leaving a 3- to 4-inch overhang on all sides.

Fill a large metal mixing bowl with ice water, and set it aside. In a medium-sized saucepan set over high heat, combine the coconut milk and condensed milk, and bring the mixture to a boil. Once the first large bubbles pop on the surface, reduce the heat and simmer, stirring constantly, until thickened, about 8 to 10 minutes. Remove the pan from the heat and stir in the lemon zest and salt.

Set the pan in the bowl of ice water and stir until the mixture is cool, about 5 minutes.

In a large mixing bowl, using an electric mixer set to medium-high, beat the cream until stiff peaks form, about 5 minutes. Gently fold the whipped cream into the coconut-milk mixture.

Stir in the chopped bourbon balls.

Pour the mixture into the prepared loaf pan, and freeze for 6 hours.

To serve, bring the dessert to room temperature, about 20 minutes. Loosen the sides with a butter knife dipped in hot water. Invert onto a serving platter, and peel away the parchment. Cut the loaf into individual slices.

Store in the freezer, wrapped tightly in plastic wrap or foil, for up to 5 days.

Grilled Bourbon-Glazed Peaches with Homemade Raspberry Sorbet

Kentucky summers mean firing up the grill and gathering loved ones in the backyard for feasts and games. As long as you're standing there sipping a cold highball, why not glaze some sweet, juicy peaches with bourbon, and toss them on the fire? It's hot out there, so cool down the liquor-drenched fruit with some tart and icy raspberry sorbet.

Makes 4 individual desserts

FOR THE SORBET
1 cup sugar
1 cup apple juice
24 ounces fresh raspberries
Juice of ½ lemon

FOR THE PEACHES
2 tablespoons butter
¼ cup light brown sugar, firmly packed
¼ cup bourbon
¼ teaspoon salt
2 large, ripe peaches, pitted and halved

TO MAKE THE SORBET
Line a 9 x 13-inch baking sheet with parchment, and set it aside.

In a medium-sized, heavy-bottomed saucepan set over medium-high heat, combine the sugar and apple juice, and bring to a boil, stirring occasionally. Reduce the heat to medium, and cook until the sugar dissolves. Remove from the heat, and let cool for 20 minutes.

Combine the cooled syrup, raspberries, and lemon juice in a blender and blend on high until you have a smooth puree, about 3 to 5 minutes.

Pour the mixture through a fine-mesh wire strainer, and discard the solids.

Pour the raspberry puree onto the prepared sheet and freeze until set. Once set, loosen the sheet of frozen puree with a butter knife, and transfer it to a clean baking sheet or a large piece of foil on the countertop.

Reline the baking sheet with parchment, and set it aside again.

Using your hands, break the frozen puree into pieces and put them into the blender again, working in batches. Blend on medium-high, until the puree is the consistency of very thick applesauce, about 2 minutes per batch.

Repeat the process of freezing and blending the puree. Once you've blended it again, serve it immediately or store it in the freezer, in a tightly lidded container, for up to 2 weeks.

TO MAKE THE GRILLED PEACHES

Light the grill.

Combine the butter, sugar, bourbon, and salt in a medium-sized saucepan. Cook on medium heat until butter and sugar are melted. Remove from heat.

Lightly toss the peaches in the sauce to coat, then leave them to marinate.

Using a grill brush, lightly coat the hot grill with canola oil. Place peaches cut side down onto grates. Turn when light grill marks appear and the peaches begin to caramelize, about 5 minutes, and cook on the other side.

Serve warm, or store in the refrigerator in a tightly lidded bowl for up to 1 week.

TO ASSEMBLE

Divide the sorbet evenly among four 8-ounce dessert cups or bowls. Lay a warm peach half on top of each, and drizzle with the remaining bourbon sauce.

❧ *Bourbon Fact*

White whiskey sure sounds better than rotgut, pop skull, or moonshine . . .

White whiskey, the latest trendy spirit, is basically moonshine. A high-proof corn liquor with a harsh finish, it's what bourbon starts out as before aging and contact with charred oak barrels mellow it.

Bourbon Blackout Sorbet

This isn't the bad kind of blackout; it's the good kind, from chocolate, with a side of bourbon. Spooning this into your mouth is kind of like biting into a rich chocolate bar, then throwing back a bourbon chaser.

Makes 1 quart

2 cups water, divided
1 cup sugar
¾ cup unsweetened cocoa powder
    (I like Scharffen Berger's)
⅛ teaspoon salt
6 ounces dark chocolate (Valrhona Le Noir Extra
    Amer 85% Cacao, if you can find it, but at least
    70% cacao), chopped
½ teaspoon pure vanilla extract
¼ cup bourbon

In a large, heavy-bottomed saucepan set over medium-high heat, whisk together 1½ cups of the water with the sugar, cocoa powder, and salt. Bring the mixture to a boil, whisking frequently. Allow it to boil for 1 minute, whisking constantly.

Remove the pan from the heat and add the chocolate, whisking until it's fully melted. Stir in the vanilla, bourbon, and the remaining ½ cup water.

Transfer the mixture to a blender and blend on high for 15 seconds. Scrape the mixture into a metal bowl, and freeze it for half an hour, then freeze it in your ice cream maker according to the manufacturer's instructions.

Store in the freezer in a tightly lidded container for up to 2 weeks.

Make Mine a Manhattan Ice Cream

⤳ A jewel-colored Manhattan cocktail in a sturdy glass with a long stem is a thing of beauty. This ice cream hits all the desirable marks of that delicious imbibable. Bourbon, cherries, vermouth, and bitters make this frozen delight as upscale and special as a fancy night out at a supper club.

The abundance of spirits in this ice cream retard the freezing process. In the end, the texture will be more semifreddo than traditional ice cream. Make it in advance and let it rest in the freezer for at least a full day, if not more.

Makes 1 quart

6 egg yolks
1½ cups whole milk
2 cups heavy cream
¼ cup sugar
½ teaspoon salt
¼ cup bourbon
2 tablespoons sweet vermouth
1 dash Angostura bitters
Whipped cream (page 122), for garnish
Maraschino cherries, for garnish
Strips of orange peel, for garnish

Put the yolks in a medium-sized heat-proof bowl and whisk, about 1 minute; set aside.

In a large, heavy-bottomed saucepan set over medium heat, combine the milk, cream, sugar, and salt and cook, stirring frequently, over medium heat.

When small bubbles form along the sides of the pan, ladle ½ cup of the milk and cream mixture into the bowl with the yolks. Whisk immediately and briskly to temper, then add another ½ cup, repeating the process.

Once the eggs are tempered, slowly whisk the egg mixture into the milk and cream mixture. Stirring constantly, cook over low heat or until the cream mixture has thickened enough to coat the back of a spoon, about 5 minutes.

Remove the pan from the heat, and stir in the bourbon, vermouth, and bitters.

Pour the mixture into a large, tightly lidded container, and refrigerate for at least 6 hours.

Freeze the mixture in an ice cream maker according to the manufacturer's instructions. Because of the alcohol, the ice cream will not freeze hard in the machine, but it will become aerated and the texture will change to that of a semifreddo.

Transfer the mixture back to the tightly lidded container and freeze for at least 4 hours before serving. To serve, scoop ice cream into martini glasses, add a dollop of whipped cream, and garnish with a cherry and an orange twist.

Store in the freezer, in the same lidded container, for up to 2 weeks.

❧ *Bourbon Fact*

Bourbon doesn't grow on trees.

The White Oak is known as the "whiskey tree" to Kentucky farmers. During fallow winter months of yore, workers who depended on the land for their sustenance spent their time productively, cutting down the trees to make the signature charred white oak barrels that give bourbon its distinctive flavor.

6   Syrups, Sauces, and Toppings

> What's your favorite part of a sundae? The syrup, of course! And there's a reason that something unexpected and extra-special is called "the icing on the cake." Syrups, sauces, frostings, and other toppings are a bonus. Whatever they enrobe would have been good enough. The added flavor, be it contrasting or complementary, generally makes it great.

I don't know about you, but I'd only eat a pile of pancakes au naturel if there was not a jar of jam or bottle of syrup in the house. And then, I'd probably slather them with melted butter and sprinkle on a bit of sugar, making my own sauce deconstruction.

Adding bourbon to this category of goodies will only make what's good, great. The recipes in this chapter all have a little somethin'-somethin' stirred in. What's always been nice has been promoted to special.

Derby Morning Maple-Bourbon Hotcake Syrup

⤳ The yield of this recipe is just enough for a large Bundt cake. When you make this syrup, however, you might want to think about doubling or even tripling that recipe. Taste one spoonful of this delicious, versatile syrup, and you'll want a gallon in your refrigerator to pour over waffles, pancakes, cornbread, and pound cake.

Makes about 2 cups

½ cup pure maple syrup
¼ cup water
1 cup vanilla sugar (page 99), or use granulated
    sugar plus 1 teaspoon pure vanilla extract
⅛ teaspoon salt
1 teaspoon butter
2 tablespoons bourbon

In a large saucepan (trust me: use a large one to avoid boil-over) over medium-high heat, bring the maple syrup, water, sugar, and salt to a boil. Once the first large bubble pops on the surface, reduce the heat, and cook for 5 minutes, stirring constantly.

Add the butter, vanilla (if using), and bourbon. Cook until the syrup thickens to the consistency of warm honey, about 5 to 7 minutes. Serve immediately.

Store in a tightly covered jar, in the refrigerator, for up to 5 days.

Honey-Kissed Bourbon Butter

⟡ Like many a native Kentuckian, I have roots in Ireland. There's a saying there that goes, "What whiskey and butter won't cure, there's no cure for." I'll buy that, but given the soil on which I was born, I'll have to respectfully replace the whiskey with bourbon.

Makes about 1 cup

¾ cup (1½ sticks) butter, at room temperature
2½ tablespoons honey
2½ tablespoons bourbon

Beat the butter with an electric hand mixer set on medium-high, or mix until smooth and fluffy, about 5 minutes. Beat in the honey a third at a time, about 30 seconds between each addition. Once amber-colored and smooth, slowly beat in the bourbon, half a tablespoon at a time, until the mixture is just combined, about 30 seconds between each addition. Transfer the mixture to a small lidded container and cover it tightly. The bourbon will leach out of the butter and float on the top, so give it a stir before serving. Keeps for 3 days stored in a cool dark place, such as the pantry. Don't refrigerate.

Tangy Bourbon–Lemon Curd Frosting

⤳ Beaten into light, creamy frosting, lemon curd finds an alternate personality as a shy but beautiful ingredient. Lemon and bourbon are a winning combination in any pastry, and topping a plain-jane cake with this spreadable treat will give it the oomph you need to make it guest-worthy.

Makes about 2 cups

1½ cups confectioners' sugar
¾ cup (1½ sticks) unsalted butter, softened
¼ cup Bourbon Lemon Curd (page 174), or use
    store bought plus 1 tablespoon bourbon
1 tablespoon whole milk (more or less, as needed)

Combine the sugar and butter in a large bowl and, using an electric mixer set on medium-high speed, beat until light and fluffy, about 3 minutes.

    Reduce the speed to low. Add the lemon curd and bourbon (if using), and beat until well combined. If the frosting is too stiff, add milk, a little at a time, beating after each addition.

    Store in the refrigerator in a tightly lidded container up to 1 month.

Run for the Roses Syrup

Anyone from Kentucky can easily call up an image of a noble horse, proudly flexing its muscles in the Winner's Circle of Churchill Downs, draped in a garland of red roses. Roses are associated with winners and triumph. Mixed with seltzer, my Run for the Roses Syrup recalls the drink offered in toast to the winners of the Abu Dhabi and Bahrain Grands Prix (used because of those countries' traditional religious prohibition against alcohol).

The fragrance and flavor of roses are prized around the globe, but I'll grant you that it's an acquired taste, like lavender or licorice.

If you're like my grandmother was, you enjoy yearly fertile and abundant rose bushes, drooping with blooms and hips. If your blossoms are grown without pesticides, you can use them to make this syrup fresh. If not, food-grade rose petals and hips are easy to find at specialty tea shops, wholesale herb companies, and sources on the web. Dried petals and hips can both be substituted, cup for cup, for fresh.

Kentucky Plus

- Drizzle syrup over Greek yogurt and sprinkle with fresh raspberries and finely chopped mint.

- Beat into softened butter to make a delicate breakfast pastry spread.

- In a tall, chilled glass, add equal parts whole milk and ice, and add 2 tablespoons of the rose syrup for a Derby-themed egg cream.

Makes about 3 cups

3 cups water
2 large handfuls fresh or dried unsprayed
    rose petals
2 handfuls fresh or dried rosehips, washed
    and coarsely chopped
1½ cups granulated sugar
Juice of ½ lemon
2 tablespoons bourbon

In a large, nonreactive pot over high heat, bring 3 cups water to a boil and add the rose petals. Turn off the heat, cover the pan with a tight lid, and let the mixture stand overnight. The next day, strain the mixture through a fine-mesh strainer into a large bowl, reserving the water and discarding the petals.

Place the rosewater back into the same pot and add the rose hips. Bring the mixture to a boil, then turn off the heat and cover with a tight lid. After an hour, strain the mixture through a colander and discard the solids, reserving the water.

Strain again through a fine-mesh strainer lined with a coffee filter or cheesecloth to remove the sediment. Transfer the strained, infused water back to the pot and, over very low heat, stir in the sugar and lemon juice, heating until the sugar dissolves but never allowing the mixture to boil. Pour into a clean, large glass jar and refrigerate for up to 3 weeks.

Orange-Bourbon Syrup for Coffee

Coffee and fresh-squeezed orange juice just say morning to me. Add a shot of bourbon, and the buffet is complete.

If you're out of OJ and booze, throw some of this gorgeously perfumed syrup into your morning cup. Don't be tempted to top it with whipped cream, though. The dairy doesn't play well with citric acid.

Makes about 2 cups

¼ cup water
1 cup fresh-squeezed orange juice without pulp
½ cup granulated sugar
¼ cup bourbon
⅛ teaspoon salt
3 whole cloves (or ¼ teaspoon ground cloves)
6 cardamom pods, split and crushed
    (or ½ teaspoon ground cardamom)

In a small bowl, combine the water and orange juice, and stir.

Put the sugar in a medium sized, heavy-bottomed saucepan set over medium-high heat, adding enough of the orange juice mixture to make it look like wet sand, about ¼ cup. Cover the pot and bring it to a boil.

Reduce the heat to medium, and cook, without stirring, until the sugar turns a dark orange-auburn color. (If you have a candy thermometer, heat to 280 degrees F.) Watch the pot closely, as sugar burns easily. Once the mixture reaches the desired temperature or color, remove the pot from the heat and let cool for 5 minutes.

Gradually pour in the rest of the orange juice mixture. (Stay alert and stand back from the stove a little; sugar mixtures can boil over in the blink of an eye.) Add the bourbon, salt, cloves, and cardamom, and stir well.

Bring the mixture to a simmer, then remove the pan from heat and let cool to room temperature. If using whole spices, fish them out with a slotted spoon and discard them.

Store in an airtight container in the refrigerator for up to 7 days.

Bourbon Fact

Yes, we have bourbon! No, I can't give you any.

Owing to local blue laws generally intended to promote community religious practices and decrease vice, Bourbon County is a "dry" county, meaning residents aren't allowed to sell any liquor.

Vanilla-Bourbon Soda Syrup

Rich, full-bodied, and bursting with vanilla and caramel flavors, this syrup tastes great mixed in a tall, ice-filled glass of seltzer. A convenient cocktail, since the bourbon's already in there. But no one says you can't add an extra shot!

Makes about 3 cups

1½ cups water
¾ cup bourbon, divided
Juice of 1 lemon
2 cups sugar
2 vanilla beans, split and scraped
⅛ teaspoon salt

In a small bowl, combine the water, ½ cup bourbon, and lemon juice.

Put the sugar in a medium-sized, heavy-bottomed saucepan set over medium-high heat, adding enough of the lemon and water mixture to make it look like wet sand, about ⅓ cup. Cover the pot and bring it to a boil.

Reduce the heat to medium, and cook, without stirring, until the sugar turns a dark brownish-auburn color. (If you have a candy thermometer,

heat to 280 degrees F.) Watch the pot closely, as sugar burns easily. Once the mixture reaches the desired temperature or color, remove the pot from the heat and let cool for 5 minutes.

Gradually pour in the rest of the lemon water. (Stay alert and stand back from the stove a little; sugar mixtures can boil over in the blink of an eye.)

Add the remaining ¼ cup bourbon, vanilla, and salt; stir well and bring the mixture to a simmer.

Remove the pan from the heat and let cool to room temperature. Fish the vanilla beans out with a slotted spoon, rinse them, and allow them to dry. (Reserve the vanilla beans to use in making vanilla sugar; see page 99.)

Store in an airtight container in the refrigerator for up to 7 days.

HARD CREAM SODA
For one drink, fill a tall glass with ice. Add 3 tablespoons of the Vanilla-Bourbon Soda Syrup. Top with seltzer and stir.

Bourbon–Apple Cider Syrup

⟩ This recipe includes a technique for a reduction. This is the way chefs distill the essence of a food, producing a concentrated flavor that's the opposite of watered down. The simplest way to describe this syrup is spicy and appley, with a healthy dose of bourbon.

Makes about 2 cups

½ gallon fresh apple cider
1 stick cinnamon
3 whole cloves
1 pinch salt
¼ cup bourbon

In a medium saucepan set over medium heat, bring the cider, cinnamon stick, cloves, and salt to a light simmer, never boiling. Cook slowly, reducing the liquid by more than half, to around 2 cups, about 60 minutes. Add the bourbon, and stir. Remove the pan from the heat and let cool.

Fish out the cinnamon stick and cloves using a slotted spoon, and discard.

Store the syrup in an airtight container in the refrigerator for up to 7 days.

HARD CIDER SODA
For one drink, fill a tall glass with ice. Add 3 tablespoons of the Bourbon–Apple Cider Syrup. Top with seltzer and stir.

VELVETY KENTUCKY NIGHT COCKTAIL
For one drink, fill a tall glass with ice. Add 3 tablespoons of the Bourbon–Apple Cider Syrup plus 1 tablespoon dark rum and 1 tablespoon pure maple syrup.

Toasted Almond and Bourbon Syrup for Cocoa

⟫ This syrup pairs naturally with hot chocolate, with its nutty flavor that just hints at bitterness and the deep oakiness provided by Kentucky bourbon.

Serve the hot blend flanked by fruit pastries or nut-based cookies, or enjoy it on its own, as I do: sitting in front of a winter's fire, wrapped in my grandma's afghan, entertaining friends and family by spinning tall tales.

Makes about 2 cups

1 cup blanched almonds
1 cup dark brown sugar, loosely packed
¼ cup bourbon
1½ cups boiling water

Preheat the oven to 350 degrees F.

Once the oven is hot, line a baking sheet or the tray of your toaster oven with foil, and spread the almonds in a single layer. Toast the nuts until golden brown, about 5 to 7 minutes. Keep a close eye on them; I've burned more than one batch by getting distracted. (Here's a hint: If you smell them, they're done.) Remove the entire pan to a wire baking rack to cool, about 15 minutes.

Once cooled, combine the almonds and the sugar in the bowl of a food processor, and pulse until ground. Take care not to overgrind, or you'll wind up with almond butter.

Transfer the mixture to a heat-proof bowl, and pour in the bourbon and boiling water. Whisk until the sugar is completely dissolved, then let the mixture cool.

Cover the bowl tightly with plastic wrap, and refrigerate overnight.

Strain the syrup through a colander lined with either cheesecloth or coffee filters. Store the syrup in an airtight container in the refrigerator for up to 7 days.

Bourbon and Sorghum Buttercream

To those unfamiliar with sorghum, let me explain. It's like a cross between brown sugar and honey, with a unique dark, malty richness. More buttery and complex than molasses and more southern than maple syrup, sorghum was once a sweetener used by poor folk and farm hands. Craft-brewers and small-batch artisan distillers are discovering this nuanced sweetener and bringing about its renaissance. Look for 100 percent pure sorghum syrup at farmer's markets, gourmet food stores, or online. Use it in this mouthwatering frosting, and use the concoction to frost about 4 dozen cupcakes, or 2 standard sheet cakes, or a three-tiered layer cake.

Makes about 5 cups frosting

2 cups (4 sticks) unsalted butter, at room temperature
6 cups confectioner's sugar, sifted
¼ cup sorghum syrup
2 tablespoons bourbon
2 tablespoons whole milk, as needed

In a large mixing bowl, using an electric mixer set to medium-high speed, beat the butter until light and fluffy, about 3 minutes. Sift in the sugar, a little at a time, beating well after each addition.

Add the sorghum syrup and beat until just incorporated, about 2 minutes.

Add the bourbon, and beat until incorporated, 1 or 2 minutes.

Depending on the consistency of your frosting at this point, add milk, ½ tablespoon at a time as needed, then continue beating until the frosting is light and fluffy.

Store in the refrigerator in a tightly lidded bowl, for up to 2 weeks.

Kentucky Bourbon Hot Fudge Sauce

This syrup stores wonderfully, so keep it in the refrigerator to warm up at a moment's notice. Serve it warm over bread pudding, waffles, sliced strawberries, or pound cake. And don't forget . . . it's always good on ice cream.

Makes about 3 cups

3 tablespoons all-purpose flour
1 cup granulated sugar
2 tablespoons unsweetened cocoa powder
    (I like Scharffen Berger's)
¼ teaspoon salt
4 tablespoons (½ stick) butter
1 cup heavy cream
1 cup half-and-half
2 tablespoons bourbon
1 teaspoon pure vanilla extract

In a large mixing bowl, whisk together the flour, sugar, cocoa powder, and salt.

In a medium-sized, heavy-bottomed saucepan set over medium-low heat, melt the butter. Gradually add the flour mixture, whisking constantly to form a smooth paste.

Slowly add the cream, half-and-half, bourbon, and vanilla, whisking thoroughly as you go. Once all the ingredients are fully incorporated, simmer gently (don't boil), still whisking constantly, until the sauce is thick and smooth, the consistency of warm honey.

Serve immediately or allow to cool before storing.

Store in the refrigerator, in a tightly lidded container, for up to 2 weeks.

 Bourbon Fact

Who said angels are teetotalers?
    In the jargon of bourbon distillers, the percentage of liquor that evaporates, or is absorbed into the wood of the barrels and is lost forever, is called "the angel's share."

Cheesy Bourbon-Buttercream Frosting

> I see mastering this frosting recipe as a "teach a man to fish"-style opportunity. Honestly, any item spread with this delicious, zingy-sour icing is instantly raised to the status of special. The combination of butter with the cream cheese mellows it, ensuring that it won't clash with other distinctive flavors. This frosting is equally at home on a pan of fudge brownies as it is on a red velvet cake. Try it on pumpkin muffins or snickerdoodles, and your guests will be clamoring to know what your secret is. Simple: it's bourbon.

Makes about 3½ cups

8 ounces cream cheese
½ cup (1 stick) butter
¼ teaspoon salt
4 cups confectioners' sugar, sifted
1½ tablespoons bourbon
2 tablespoons whole milk, as needed

In a large mixing bowl, using an electric mixer set on medium-high speed, combine the cream cheese, butter, and salt until light and fluffy, about 3 minutes.

Reduce the speed to low, and gradually add in the confectioners' sugar, beating well after each addition, about 2 minutes.

Add the bourbon, half a tablespoon at a time, and beat on low after each addition until it's just blended, about 1 minute. If the frosting is too stiff, add milk, 1 teaspoon at a time, beating well after each addition, until it's smooth and spreadable.

Kentucky Plus

> Use this frosting as the cream filling in a carrot-cake whoopee pie recipe.

> For Bourbon and Chocolate Cream Cheese Frosting, add ½ cup unsweetened cocoa powder, beating it in with the confectioners' sugar.

7 Candies

My Grandma Rose was a hairdresser from the time she was fifteen, when she quit the Ursuline Academy for Girls to ride the streetcar downtown in order to apprentice at a beauty shop in Louisville's glamorous Starks Building. This meant she always had her own money, and she spent it how she liked. People like that are hard to buy gifts for, but one surefire hit for her birthday or Mother's Day was a box of Modjeskas, otherwise known as Caramel Biscuits, from Muth's candy store, situated not too far from the banks of the Ohio River. Individually wrapped candies, consisting of soft caramel enrobing homemade marshmallow squares, Modjeskas are said to have been named after Helena Modjeska, a Polish star of the stage, who visited Louisville to perform at the McCauley Theatre.

My mother knew how to wow my grandmother, too. She'd make a homemade batch of bourbon balls that Grandma Rose declared the best in Louisville.

A true fan of candy—homemade or otherwise—and a doting grandmother, she also never failed to heap praise on my offerings of canned peanut brittle and packaged circus peanuts bought at the drugstore with my piggy-bank money.

If Grandma Rose were with me today, I'd whip up a batch of each of the candies in this chapter. She loved bourbon, and she loved candy. I know it would make her smile.

Betty Lou's Bourbon Balls

My mother never made a dozen or so bourbon balls; she made legions of them. I always thought it was because so many members of our huge extended family were begging her for heavy tins full of the boozy confections. This is probably true. My mother's bourbon balls were legendary, and the appreciation for them was ample.

After my first attempt to make them, a light dawned. It's a time-consuming production, requiring focus, speed, and labor. Don't let that scare you off, though. The difficulty level is low; anyone can do it. But my theory (and I suspect my mom's) was that as long as you're making a dozen, you may as well make twelve dozen.

Some people add paraffin to help set the chocolate, but my mother used patience and perseverance instead, working in small batches and availing herself of the refrigerator's chilling properties. Don't make these in a hot kitchen! A college roommate and I attempted it, and we were wiping chocolate smudges off the walls, floors, and even cats, for months.

Makes about 4 dozen

½ cup (1 stick) butter, at room temperature
2 cups confectioners' sugar
5 tablespoons bourbon
1 teaspoon vanilla
¾ cup coarsely chopped pecans
12 ounces semisweet chocolate chips, divided
Whole pecans, for garnish

In a large mixing bowl, stir together the butter, confectioners' sugar, bourbon, and vanilla using a fork, until smooth.

Cover the bowl, and chill in the refrigerator for 8 hours, or overnight.

Roll the candy into 1-inch balls, working as quickly as possible so you don't melt the candy cream with the heat of your hands, and transfer them to zip-top freezer bags. Lay them flat, in a single layer, and freeze for another 8 hours, or overnight.

Line four 9 x 13-inch baking sheets with waxed paper. Take half of the frozen nougat balls out of the freezer and set them aside on the countertop.

Put half of the chocolate chips in a large, microwavable bowl and heat on high for 90 seconds. Remove and stir well. Let the chips rest for a minute or two, stirring often. The residual heat will continue to melt them. If more time is needed, microwave in 10-second bursts, stirring well after each. (If you continuously microwave the chocolate without stirring and resting, you may scorch it.)

Working quickly, spear the balls one by one with a toothpick, and carefully dip each into the melted chocolate. After each dip, tap the toothpick against the side of the bowl to knock off the excess chocolate. Set the coated ball on a prepared baking sheet. Using another toothpick, push the bourbon ball gently from the toothpick. Cover the toothpick mark with a pecan half.

Set the first half of the candies in the refrigerator to chill, and repeat the process with the second half.

Store in a cool, dark place, in a tightly sealed candy tin, for up to 1 month. (I store mine in the refrigerator or freezer to keep them from melting.)

Paw Paw's Tavern Caramels

❧ A block from my grandparents' house on Mulberry Street, in the Schnitzelberg section of Germantown, there was a tavern called the White Cottage Saloon. It's what I now call an "old man bar." At one time, nearly every block in that part of Louisville was home to a tavern just like it. Always cool, always dark, you could get a ham sandwich on rye wrapped in waxed paper or a pickled egg any time of day. On the bar, there was always a jar of hard pretzels, sold for a nickel. As a kid, I couldn't decide if I liked them or not. They were hard to break into pieces, and they squeaked in your teeth when you chewed. Today, I'd give anything to kill half an hour working my way through one of those pretzels, sitting next to my Paw Paw as he contentedly nursed his beer and shot. Featuring pretzels, beer, and bourbon, this recipe is a tribute to his memory. A tip: These are soft caramels and must be wrapped in square, waxed-paper packages like Modjeska candies, or they'll run.

Makes about 75 one-inch pieces

1 (12-ounce) bottle nut brown ale, divided
4 ounces bourbon
2 cups granulated sugar
1 cup dark brown sugar, packed
1 cup (2 sticks) butter, plus more for greasing pan
1 cup heavy cream
1 cup light corn syrup
1 (8-ounce) package pretzel rods

Line a 9 x 13-inch pan with parchment, leaving a 3-inch overhang on all sides.

In a small, heavy-bottomed saucepan, bring 1 cup of the ale and the bourbon to a boil. Reduce the heat and simmer gently until the liquid reduces to a very small amount of concentrated syrup (about 2 tablespoons), about 20 to 30 minutes. When you think you cannot reduce the syrup any more, reduce it a little more. Set aside.

Combine remaining ale, granulated sugar, brown sugar, butter, cream, and corn syrup in a large, heavy-bottomed pot set over medium heat, with a candy or frying thermometer affixed to the side. Cook, stirring occasionally, until the butter melts and large bubbles pop on the surface. At this stage, stir continuously to avoid burning.

Continue to cook until a candy thermometer reaches 244 degrees F, about 30 minutes. (You are looking for a firm ball; you can test the consistency by dropping a bit of the caramel into a bowl of ice water. If too soft, continue cooking.)

Once done, stir in the ale-bourbon reduction, and remove the pot from the heat.

Pour the caramel into the prepared pan and lay pretzel rods in rows along the top; then refrigerate until firm.

Use the parchment to lift the chilled caramel block from pan, and flip it to pretzel-side up on a cutting board. Cut lengthwise between the pretzels (so that a rod runs through the middle of each candy square) and then crosswise into 1-inch pieces. Wrap each individual piece in waxed paper, like wrapping a present in a square box.

Store in the refrigerator for up to 1 month. Bring to room temperature before serving.

❧ *Bourbon Fact*

I know art when I see it . . .

The Oscar Getz Museum of Whiskey History, located in Spalding Hall at the Bardstown Historical Museum, boasts a fifty-year collection of rare whiskey artifacts dating from pre-colonial to post-Prohibition days. The collection includes rare antique bottles, a moonshine still, historical ad art, and novelty whiskey containers.

Bourbon-Bacon Bark

In the past few years, there's been a spike in interest in all things do-it-yourself and in the practices of the domestic arts. Basic foods and flavors have come to the fore, along with a celebration of what's simple and basic, and made by hand. To me, this bark fits in beautifully with the renewed interest in crafting. The bacon and bourbon add a modern twist to a traditional type of candy, bringing it up to date without trying too hard.

Makes 64 one-inch pieces

FOR THE CHOCOLATE-MARSHMALLOW LAYER
18 ounces semisweet chocolate chips, divided
5 cups mini marshmallows
¼ cup bourbon, divided

FOR THE SPICY BACON LAYER
1 pound bacon strips
¼ cup light brown sugar, packed
4 tablespoons water
1 large egg white
¼ teaspoon black pepper, coarsely ground
⅛ teaspoon salt
⅛ teaspoon chili powder

FOR THE VANILLA CARAMEL LAYER
1 cup granulated sugar
4 tablespoons water
4 tablespoons (½ stick) butter
7 tablespoons heavy cream
½ teaspoon vanilla

TO MAKE THE CHOCOLATE-MARSHMALLOW LAYER
Line an 8 x 8-inch glass baking dish with parchment, leaving a 3-inch overhang on all sides.

Put half of the chocolate chips in a large, microwavable bowl and heat on high for 90 seconds. Remove and stir well. Let the chips rest for a minute or two, stirring often. The residual heat will continue to melt them. If more time is needed, microwave in 10-second bursts, stirring well after each. (If you continuously microwave the chocolate without stirring and resting, you may scorch it.)

Pour the melted chocolate into the parchment-lined pan, and use a spatula to spread into a smooth, even layer. Transfer the pan to the freezer to chill for at least 15 minutes, or until the chocolate solidifies.

Put the mini marshmallows in a large, heavy-bottomed saucepan set over medium-high heat.

Cook until they melt and web-like strands form when stirred.

Remove the pan from the heat and add half of the bourbon, stirring until combined. Using a rubber spatula sprayed with nonstick spray, spread the marshmallow mixture over the chocolate layer.

TO MAKE THE SPICY BACON LAYER
Preheat the oven to 325 degrees F. Line a 9 x 13-inch baking sheet with parchment.

Fry the bacon, and let it drain and cool on layers of brown paper (laying it on paper towels will make it soggy).

Once cooled, crumble it into a small bowl, and set it aside.

In a small saucepan, over high heat, bring the sugar and water to a boil, and cook until it reduces to a simple syrup, about 5 to 8 minutes.

Transfer the bacon to a colander lined with coffee filters or cheesecloth, set in the sink. Slowly drizzle the simple syrup over the bacon, coating it evenly and thoroughly. Once all of the syrup has been used, let the bacon rest in the colander to drain off the excess.

In a medium-sized mixing bowl, beat the egg white with a fork until light and foamy. Add the black pepper, salt, and chili powder, and beat with a fork to combine. Add the bacon, and toss.

Spread the bacon onto the prepared pan, and bake for 20 minutes, until browned and crispy. Remove from the oven and set the pan on a wire rack to cool.

TO MAKE THE VANILLA CARAMEL LAYER
Combine the sugar and water in a medium-sized, heavy-bottomed saucepan set over medium-low heat. Stir occasionally until sugar has dissolved, forming a simple syrup, about 5 to 8 minutes.

Increase the heat to high and swirl the pan constantly, until the sugar turns reddish-amber, about 5 minutes. Sugar burns easily, so keep swirling!

Gradually add the butter, cream, and vanilla, and then the remaining bourbon, now whisking constantly. Cook for 3 more minutes, until smooth and uniform. Remove the pan from the heat and set aside to cool.

TO ASSEMBLE
Slowly and evenly pour the cooled caramel over the marshmallow layer, and spread evenly, using a rubber spatula sprayed with nonstick spray.

Freeze for 15 minutes, or until the caramel has hardened.

Melt the remaining half of the chocolate chips, following the instructions above, and pour over the caramel layer, spreading it evenly with a rubber spatula.

Evenly distribute the bacon over the top of the soft chocolate, and press it down gently, using the palm of your hand. Chill in the refrigerator for 30 minutes before cutting and serving. Use the parchment to lift the bark out of the pan, then cut the candy into 64 squares.

Store in the refrigerator, tightly wrapped, with plastic wrap or foil, for up to 3 days.

❧ *Bourbon Fact*

With bourbon, you know what you're getting . . .
Bourbon's spirit production process is the most tightly regulated in the world.

Microwave Bourbon-Pecan Fudge

> When a pair of my foodie friends told me that they'd made the best fudge they'd ever eaten, and it was made in the microwave, I was skeptical. Sure, I like a shortcut, but not if it's a gateway to low-rent taste and flavor. Well, let me tell you, my objections froze in their tracks the minute my friends passed chunks of their microwave candy out to my husband, my kids, and me. Everyone involuntarily closed his or her eyes, sinking into a reverie, and cooed appreciative noises. My cooing was the loudest of all. With my friends' input, we tinkered with the recipe and added nuts and bourbon. One word: sublime.

Makes 64 one-inch squares

18 ounces semisweet chocolate chips
1 (14-ounce) can sweetened condensed milk
½ teaspoon salt
2 teaspoons vanilla
2 teaspoons bourbon
2 cups chopped pecans

Line an 8 x 8-inch glass baking dish with waxed paper, leaving a 3-inch overhang on every side.

Put the chocolate chips in a large, microwavable bowl and heat on high for 90 seconds. Remove and stir well. Let the chips rest for a minute or two, stirring often. The residual heat will continue to melt them. If more time is needed, microwave in 10-second bursts, stirring well after each. (If you continuously microwave the chocolate without stirring and resting, you may scorch it.)

Add the sweetened condensed milk, salt, vanilla, and bourbon, and beat with a fork or a whisk until smooth. Stir in the chopped nuts, and turn the mixture into the prepared pan. Refrigerate until firm, about 1 hour. Use the waxed paper overhang to lift the fudge out of the pan onto a cutting board, and cut it into 8 slices by 8 slices to make 64 small squares. Store between sheets of waxed paper in an airtight container in the refrigerator for up to 1 week.

"Kentucky after Dark" Peanut Butter Cups

⟫ As much as I love highbrow food of nearly every stripe, I'll freely admit that each year I wait for Halloween to roll around so I'll have an excuse to buy Reese's Peanut Butter Cups. I don't even lie and say they're for the kids.

This got me to thinking, "Could peanut butter cups *be* any better?"

The answer is yes. Yes, they can. Bourbon makes everything better.

Makes 12 candies

18 ounces dark chocolate chips (I like Ghirardelli)
3 tablespoons vegetable shortening
3 tablespoons bourbon
1½ cups confectioners' sugar
1 cup creamy natural peanut butter (do not use whipped and sugared brands)
½ teaspoon salt
¼ cup (½ stick) butter, at room temperature

Line a 12-cup muffin tin with brown paper baking cups.

Put the chocolate chips, shortening, and bourbon in a large, microwavable bowl and heat on high for 90 seconds. Remove and stir well. Let the mixture rest for a minute or two, stirring often. The residual heat will continue to melt the chocolate. If more time is needed, microwave in 10-second bursts, stirring well after each. (If you continuously microwave chocolate without stirring and resting, you may scorch it.)

Set the mixture aside to cool slightly, about 10 minutes, until it has a warm-honey consistency.

Drizzle a tablespoon of the chocolate into each cup, about halfway up the sides. Refrigerate for 20 minutes, until the chocolate is firm.

In a medium-sized mixing bowl, combine the confectioners' sugar, peanut butter, salt, and butter, mixing with a fork until smooth, about 5 to 7 minutes.

Remove the muffin tin from the refrigerator, and spoon about a tablespoon of the peanut butter mixture into the center of each cup, and press down gently with the back of a spoon, taking care not to spread the mixture all the way to the edges. (It will become a filling, as with fruit puree in a pie crust.)

Now, spoon about a tablespoon of the remaining chocolate mixture over the peanut butter mixture (melt in the microwave for one or two 10-second bursts if needed), allowing the chocolate to cover it on all sides and across the top.

Chill for 3 hours, or until firm.

Vanilla-Bourbon Marshmallows

Until about ten years ago, I didn't even know there was such a thing as homemade marshmallows! Somehow I must have missed them in the glass cases of Dundee Candy and Muth's. Suddenly, twenty-dollar boxes of the pillowy soft, sugar-dusted morsels began showing up in très fancy New York specialty groceries.

Once I took stock of all the various flavors used to elevate the humble confection, I rolled up my sleeves and learned how to make them, using bourbon.

Makes about 12 large or 16 small marshmallow squares

3 (¼-ounce) packages unflavored gelatin
¾ cups cold water, divided
2 cups vanilla sugar (page 99) or use granulated
    sugar plus 1 teaspoon pure vanilla extract
⅔ cup light corn syrup
1 vanilla bean, split and scraped (page 99)
2 teaspoons bourbon
¼ teaspoon coarse salt
Butter, for coating hands
Confectioners' sugar, sifted, for coating

Coat an 8 x 8-inch glass baking pan with nonstick spray. Line the pan with plastic wrap, leaving a 3-inch overhang on all sides.

In the bowl of an electric stand mixer affixed with the whisk attachment, combine the gelatin and ½ cup water, and let stand on the countertop for 15 minutes.

In a medium-sized, heavy-bottomed saucepan, set over medium-high heat, combine the sugar, corn syrup, and the remaining ¼ cup water. Bring to a rapid boil and cook, stirring constantly, for 1 minute.

Remove the pan from the heat and, with the mixer set to high, slowly add the syrup to the gelatin by drizzling it down the side of the bowl. Add salt and continue mixing for 15 minutes.

Add the vanilla extract (if using), vanilla seeds and scrapings, and bourbon. (Reserve the vanilla bean pod to use in making vanilla sugar; see page 99.) Continue mixing on high until combined.

Lightly coat your clean hands with butter, and spread the mixture into the prepared pan, smoothing and evening out the top.

Wash your hands with soap and warm water; then spray a sheet of plastic wrap with cooking spray and lay it spray-side down on top of the mixture. Let it stand in a cool, dry place for 4 hours.

Put the sifted confectioners' sugar into a deep mixing bowl, cover it with a clean dish towel, and set it aside.

Holding the overhang of the plastic wrap, gently remove marshmallow slab from the pan. Peel off and discard the plastic wrap.

Using a sharp chef's knife sprayed with non-stick spray, cut the marshmallow into squares.

Working in small batches, drench the marshmallows in the prepared bowl of sugar, and coat evenly before serving.

Store in an airtight container for up to 5 days.

Maple Leaf Marshmallow S'mores

❧   A Maple Leaf is a whisky cocktail featuring, you guessed it, maple syrup and whiskey. Cinnamon and lemon round out the flavor profile. These marshmallow s'mores shine with all the flavors of the namesake cocktail, and up the ante with the flavors of traditional campfire s'mores. Fun to build, fun to eat, this is a great interactive dessert for fun-loving grown-ups. Think dinner parties and date nights.

Makes 8

3 (¼-ounce) packages unflavored gelatin
½ cup water
2 cups granulated sugar
⅓ cup light corn syrup
⅓ cup pure maple syrup
¼ cup bourbon, plus 1 tablespoon, divided
¼ teaspoon cinnamon
1 teaspoon lemon juice
¼ teaspoon salt
Butter, for coating hands
Confectioners' sugar, sifted, for coating
4 ounces bittersweet chocolate (60% cacao), chopped
½ cup heavy cream
8 graham cracker rectangles, halved

Coat an 8 x 8-inch glass baking pan with nonstick spray. Line the pan with plastic wrap, leaving a 3-inch overhang on all sides.

In the bowl of an electric stand mixer affixed with the whisk attachment, combine the gelatin and ½ cup water, and let stand on the countertop for 15 minutes

In a medium-sized, heavy-bottomed saucepan set over medium-high heat, combine the sugar, corn syrup, maple syrup, and ¼ cup bourbon. Bring to a rapid boil, stirring constantly, and cook for 1 minute.

Remove the pan from the heat and, with the mixer set to high, slowly add the syrup to the gelatin by drizzling it down the side of the bowl. Add salt and continue mixing for 15 minutes.

Stir in the remaining tablespoon of bourbon, cinnamon, and lemon juice.

Lightly coat your clean hands with butter, and spread the mixture into the prepared pan, smoothing and evening out the top.

Wash your hands with soap and warm water; then spray a sheet of plastic wrap with cooking spray and lay it spray-side down on top of the mixture. Let it stand in a cool, dry place for 4 hours.

Put the sifted confectioners' sugar into a deep mixing bowl, cover it with a clean dish towel, and set it aside.

Holding the overhang of the plastic wrap, gently remove the marshmallow slab from the pan. Peel off and discard the plastic wrap.

Using a sharp chef's knife sprayed with non-stick spray, cut the marshmallow into 8 squares.

Working in small batches, drench the marshmallows in the prepared bowl of sugar, and coat evenly.

Line a baking sheet with parchment. Put the chocolate in a large, heat-proof bowl.

In a small saucepan over medium-high heat, warm the cream just until tiny bubbles form at the edge of the pan.

Meanwhile, arrange 8 of the graham cracker halves, top side down, on the prepared baking sheet, and lay a marshmallow in the center of each. Pour the hot cream over the chocolate and whisk constantly until melted and smooth. Spoon half a tablespoon of melted chocolate mixture over each marshmallow, top with another cracker, and serve warm.

Store in a tightly lidded container on the countertop for up to 3 days. Microwave to melt the chocolate and marshmallow before serving.

Kentucky Plus

> For a salty-sweet treat, lay a strip of well-drained, crispy bacon on top of the dipped marshmallow before topping with the graham cracker.

> Spread the crackers with natural, chunky peanut butter for a tin roof s'more.

Bourbon-Sugared Pecans

⟫ Whatever happened to candy dishes? I suppose back in the day, people did such hard manual labor, in the fields, in the factories, and in the laundry rooms, that extra bumps of sugar didn't pack on the pounds. At some point, it seems, the open enjoyment of food fell by the wayside. I love to serve these at the cocktail hour. Sure, I automatically put out the olives, cheese board, and pretzel nibs, but it's a pleasure to watch grown men pop these sweetened nuts into their mouths, moan appreciatively, then wash them down with a bourbon on the rocks.

Makes 4 cups

Butter, for greasing pan
1 egg white
2 teaspoons water
1 teaspoon pure vanilla extract
2 tablespoons bourbon
4 cups (about 1 pound) pecan halves
1 cup granulated sugar
1 teaspoon kosher salt
½ teaspoon ground cinnamon
½ teaspoon freshly grated nutmeg

Preheat the oven to 300 degrees F.

Lightly butter a rimmed 9 x 13-inch baking sheet.

In a large bowl, vigorously whisk the egg white, water, vanilla, and bourbon until foamy. Add the pecans and stir so they are well coated with egg white. Working quickly, add the sugar, salt, cinnamon, and nutmeg, and toss well to coat.

Immediately spread the sugary pecans onto the prepared baking sheet. Try to work fast to prevent the sugar from completely dissolving in the egg white. Bake the pecans for 30 minutes, stirring and turning them occasionally, until they are golden brown, toasted, and completely dry, no longer wet from egg white. Cool them completely, and break any clusters into individual nuts if necessary.

Store the nuts in an airtight container at room temperature for up to 2 weeks.

Bourbon Walnut Penuche

Traditional penuche is a fudge-like candy made with brown sugar, butter, and milk, and flavored solely with vanilla. It's so basic, rich, and creamy, it's practically mother's milk. Here's my riff on penuche, with a modern texture and the flavor of bourbon.

Makes 40 pieces

3 cups light brown sugar, packed
¼ teaspoon salt
1 cup heavy cream
2 tablespoons butter, plus more for greasing pan
1 tablespoon bourbon
1½ cups finely chopped walnuts

Butter a 9 x 13-inch glass baking dish.

In a medium-sized, heavy-bottomed saucepan set over medium-high heat, with a frying or candy thermometer affixed to the side, combine the brown sugar, salt, and cream. Cook, stirring constantly, until the temperature reaches 236 degrees F, about 30 minutes. (You are looking for a soft ball; you can test the consistency by dropping a bit of the caramel into a bowl of ice water. If too soft, continue cooking.)

Remove the pan from the heat and stir in the butter; then let the mixture cool slightly, about 15 minutes. Add the bourbon and whisk vigorously by hand until the mixture loses its sheen.

Stir in the nuts and spread the soft penuche into the prepared baking dish, smoothing the top with a spatula coated with nonstick spray. Chill in the refrigerator for at least an hour before cutting into squares and removing from pan.

Store, layered between sheets of parchment, in an airtight container in the refrigerator for up to 1 week.

Coffee-and-Bourbon Pralines

> Coffee and bourbon. What a great way to start a lazy winter's day, when there's little to do but read the paper and putter around the house in your cozy socks. I love those flavors in this satisfying southern candy, and there's no law saying you can't eat them along with your steaming spiked java.

When making these pralines, use a heavy Dutch oven, and unless you're an expert, I urge you to rely on a candy thermometer. Last tip: I was taught by a true country cook that one should never make pralines when it's raining; the humidity makes them grainy.

Makes about 32

2 cups pecan halves and pieces
3 cups dark brown sugar, packed
1 tablespoon instant coffee crystals
¼ cup bourbon
1 cup heavy cream
¼ cup (½ stick) butter
2 tablespoons light corn syrup
1 teaspoon pure vanilla extract

Kentucky Plus

> For a spicier candy, add 1 teaspoon ground cinnamon and ½ teaspoon ground cloves when boiling the brown sugar.

> Not a coffee drinker? Leave it out and add an extra 2 tablespoons of bourbon.

Preheat the oven to 350 degrees F. Lay two long sheets of waxed paper on the countertop.

Arrange the pecans in a single layer on an ungreased rimmed baking sheet and bake for 8 to 10 minutes, or until toasted and fragrant, stirring once. Remove from the oven and set the baking sheet on a wire rack to cool, about 15 minutes.

Meanwhile, over medium heat and stirring constantly, bring the brown sugar, coffee crystals, bourbon, cream, butter, and corn syrup to a boil in a heavy Dutch oven affixed with a frying or candy thermometer.

Continue to cook and stir, about 8 to 10 minutes, or until the candy thermometer reads 236 degrees F. (You are looking for a soft ball; you can test the consistency by dropping a bit of the candy into a bowl of ice water. If it's too soft, continue cooking.)

Once done, remove the mixture from the heat, and let it cool until the thermometer reads 150 degrees, about 20 minutes.

Stir in the vanilla and nuts, and continue to stir briskly, until the mixture loses its sheen, about 3 minutes. Drop the candy by tablespoons onto the wax paper, leaving 2 inches between dollops.

Let stand until firm, then serve.

Store, layered between sheets of parchment, in an airtight container in the refrigerator for up to 1 week.

Simple Microwave Peanut Brittle with Bourbon

⟫ My grandmother had an odd storage cabinet above her kitchen table. It was very deep, always dark, and you had to climb onto the table to get in there. Good luck finding anything without a flashlight. She called it "The Hole." You'd think such an ominous name would deter a kid, but it didn't. I knew what was in there: boxes of assorted varieties of Christmas cookies made by her beauty-shop customers, tins of fruitcake being soaked with bourbon, and cans of peanut brittle, her favorite candy.

Makes 1 pound

1 cup salted peanuts
1 cup granulated sugar
½ cup light corn syrup
4 tablespoons (½ stick) butter, plus more for
    greasing pan
1 teaspoon pure vanilla extract
2 tablespoons bourbon
1 teaspoon baking soda

Kentucky Plus

⟫ Substitute whole salted almonds, whole salted cashews, or macadamia nut pieces in equal parts for peanuts to make conversation-piece nut brittles.

⟫ To heat things up, stir in 1 teaspoon ground cinnamon and ½ teaspoon ground cayenne pepper with the butter, vanilla, and bourbon.

Lightly butter a rimmed 9 x 13-inch baking sheet; set it aside.

In a medium, microwavable bowl, stir together the peanuts, sugar, and corn syrup. Microwave for 4 minutes on high. Stir well, then cook for 3 more minutes.

Add the butter, vanilla, and bourbon, stirring until the butter is melted.

Microwave for 90 seconds more, until the mixture is very hot. It may bubble a little. Add the baking soda, and stir to combine. (Be careful not to splash; hot sugar burns!) Don't be alarmed when the mixture foams; just keep stirring until the foam subsides.

Pour the mixture onto the prepared baking sheet and smooth it out, using a heat-proof silicone spatula coated with nonstick spray.

Let it cool at room temperature for 1 hour, or until the brittle is set. If it isn't entirely cool, freeze it for 10 minutes. (Don't be tempted to refrigerate or freeze for the whole cooling period; the air in the refrigerator is humid, and the brittle won't harden.)

Use your hands to break the sheet of peanut brittle into bite-size pieces before serving.

Store in an airtight container for up to 1 week.

❧ *Bourbon Fact*

North or South, they all agreed on bourbon.

During the Civil War, army commanders often planned routes that would enable the soldiers to camp near distilleries. As a divided state in the Civil War, Kentucky distillers would often see Union troops and Confederate troops on successive nights.

Sweet and Boozy Graham Cracker Candies

❧ I'm just going to say it: you don't get much more decadent than this candy. Filled with butter to slicken the lips, spiked with bourbon for a grown-up fizz, rich with chewy nuts, and oh so sweet.

I wrestle with whether it's a toffee, a praline, or a caramel. As they say, a rose by any other name would be just as tooth-stickingly sweet and boozy.

Makes 36 pieces

1 package graham crackers (9 rectangles)
½ cup whole pecans
½ cup (1 stick) butter
½ cup light brown sugar
Pinch of salt
1½ tablespoons bourbon

Preheat the oven to 350 degrees F.

Line a 9 x 13-inch baking sheet with parchment.

Break each cracker into four small rectangles and set them on the baking sheet. Top each with a pecan.

In a medium saucepan over medium-high heat, melt the butter and sugar together, stirring constantly. Add the pinch of salt and continue to stir until the mixture comes to a full rolling boil. Add the bourbon, and stir until combined.

Spoon the butter-sugar mixture over the graham crackers. Bake for 10 minutes, or until the entire pan is bubbling. Remove from the oven, set the pan on a wire rack, and leave to cool and set at room temperature.

When the toffee is completely set, break the crackers into individual pieces. They will come out as whole rectangles, with a crisp sheet of toffee around the edges of each piece. Layer the crackers between sheets of waxed paper and store in an airtight container at room temperature for up to 1 week.

8

Compotes, Chutneys, Spreads, and Preserves

❧ Something homemade in a jar, with a square of gingham on the top, tied up with a fresh ribbon. Now that is a gift that says, "I care."

Everyone who puts up preserves adds his or her own particular spin. More or less sugar. A particular blend of fruits. A proprietary combination of spices. It never stops being fun to try someone else's.

A useful gift is a thoughtful gift, and jam, jellies, preserves, and chutneys never go to waste. Spread them on toast, use them to fill tarts or thumbprint cookies, spoon them over ice cream, or put a dollop on a stack of flapjacks. They breathe new life into foods you thought you had already met.

The fruit dishes and spreads in this chapter are united by a common thread: bourbon. Delicious to begin with, each and every one enjoys its new moment in the sun, flaunting this "everything old is new again" ingredient.

Dried-Fruit Compote with Bourbon Custard

❧ I love fruit compote for its historical quality. It seems like something they'd have eaten at Locust Grove, Louisville's most famous historical home and museum, or at the dinner table of Claudia Sanders, owner of The Dinner House in Shelbyville, Kentucky, and wife of the first gentleman of Kentucky-style fried chicken, Colonel Sanders. I feel similarly about custard, which I link in my mind with steamed puddings. And don't forget, in "olden days" people had no compunction about throwing a splash or two of liquor into their desserts. For medicinal purposes, of course.

Once you get the hang of this recipe, I urge you to branch out and experiment with different dried fruits, making it your signature dish. When you're itchy to switch up the dessert menu from cakes and pies, this is a great meal capper to try.

Makes 4 individual desserts

FOR THE CUSTARD
2 cups heavy cream
⅓ cup vanilla sugar (page 99), or use granulated sugar and add ½ teaspoon pure vanilla extract
5 egg yolks
1 tablespoon cornstarch

FOR THE FRUIT COMPOTE
¼ cup water
½ cup orange juice
2 tablespoons granulated sugar
1 stick cinnamon
1½ vanilla beans, split lengthwise and scraped
½ cup dried apricots
½ cup dried apples
½ cup dried figs, halved

TO MAKE THE CUSTARD
In a medium-sized, heavy-bottomed saucepan set over medium-high heat, combine the cream and the ½ teaspoon vanilla, if using, and bring it to a light simmer, stirring occasionally, just until tiny bubbles form at the edges.

Remove the pan from the heat and set it aside.

In a medium-sized, heat-proof bowl, combine the egg yolks, sugar, and cornstarch, and whisk to combine.

Add about half a cup of the warm cream mixture to the egg mixture, and whisk to temper. Gradually add the rest of the cream mixture, whisking continuously.

Return the custard mixture to the saucepan and cook over low heat for 5 to 7 minutes, or until the mixture is thickened and coats the back of a spoon. Serve warm with the fruit.

TO MAKE THE COMPOTE

In a medium-sized saucepan set over medium heat, combine the water, juice, sugar, cinnamon stick, and vanilla seeds and scrapings, and stir until sugar is dissolved. (Reserve the vanilla bean pod to use in making vanilla sugar; see page 99.)

Add the apricots, apples, and figs and bring the mixture to a boil.

Reduce heat to low, and simmer gently for 5 to 7 minutes. Using a slotted spoon, remove the cinnamon stick, and remove the pan from the heat.

TO ASSEMBLE

Divide the fruit among four 6- to 8-ounce ramekins or dessert bowls. Spoon the custard over the ramekins, and serve warm.

Store the custard and the compote in separate, tightly lidded containers in the refrigerator; the custard will keep for up to 5 days; the compote will keep for up to 2 weeks.

Boozetella

A jar of concentrated, spreadable chocolate: mmm. Concentrated, spreadable chocolate with bourbon in it: mind-blowing. Be like me, and pretend that this is sort of healthy, like peanut butter or cream cheese, and deny the fact that it's spreadable candy with a touch of booze. You'll almost feel virtuous when you slather it on toast.

Makes about 2 pint jars

1 cup raw hazelnuts
12 ounces bittersweet chocolate chips
2½ tablespoons canola oil
3 tablespoons confectioners' sugar
1 tablespoon unsweetened cocoa powder
  (I like Scharffen Berger's)
2 tablespoons bourbon
½ teaspoon vanilla extract
½ teaspoon salt

Preheat the oven to 350 degrees F.

Once the oven is hot, line a baking sheet or the tray of your toaster oven with foil, and spread the hazelnuts in a single layer. Toast the nuts until they have darkened to a deep golden brown and the skins have blistered, about 12 to 14 minutes. Keep a close eye on them; I've burned more than one batch by getting distracted. (Here's a hint: If you smell them, they're done.)

Remove from the oven, set the baking sheet on a wire rack, and let cool slightly.

Wrap the nuts in a clean dish towel, and rub to remove as much of the skin as possible. Use your fingers to pull off any large pieces, but don't worry if some skin clings. Let the nuts cool completely, about 30 minutes.

Put the chocolate chips in a large, microwavable bowl and heat on high for 90 seconds. Remove and stir well. Let the chips rest for a minute or two, stirring often. The residual heat will continue to melt them. If more time is needed, microwave in 10-second bursts, stirring well after each. (If you continuously microwave the chocolate without stirring and resting, you may scorch it.)

Once the chocolate is fully melted, stir until smooth and let cool slightly.

Put the hazelnuts in the bowl of a food processor, and process in bursts until they form a paste, about 7 to 10 minutes.

Add the oil, sugar, cocoa powder, bourbon, vanilla, and salt. Continue to process the mixture until the mixture is as smooth as possible, about 7 to 10 minutes.

Add the melted chocolate and continue to blend until smooth and well combined, about 3 to 5 minutes.

Transfer the spread into clean pint jars, and allow to cool on the countertop.

Store, covered in the jars, in a cool, dark place for up to 2 weeks.

Kentucky Plus

❯ For an even nuttier spread, substitute hazelnut or peanut oil for the canola oil

❯ Use as a filling in Thumbprint Cookies (page 52).

❯ Slather a slice of white bread with Boozetella, and another with marshmallow fluff, and put a banana in between for a sandwich Elvis might have loved.

Bourbon-Cherry Jam

❧ Bourbon and cherries should be in love and get married. Both are sweet, deep, folksy, and fragrant. And yet they're so different. Isn't that what being a couple is all about?

I'm offering this in a small batch, so you don't have to worry about canning it properly. If your house is anything like mine, it won't last long enough to store in the root cellar, anyway. Some jams use pectin to help the set. It's my assertion that cherry jam is supposed to be a bit more loose and syrupy, so I rely on the pectin offered naturally by the fruit and the chill of the refrigerator for the right consistency.

Makes about 3 pint jars

3 pounds sweet cherries, pitted
3 cups granulated sugar
2 tablespoons lemon juice
3 tablespoons bourbon

Put four tablespoons in the freezer to chill. You'll use at least one of these to perform the "spoon test" for doneness (see below).

In a stockpot over medium heat, combine the cherries, sugar, and lemon juice, and toss with a

❧ The Tried-and-True Spoon Test for Preserves

To check for the "doneness" of preserves, ladle a teaspoon of jam into a frozen tablespoon. (Do not dip the frozen spoon into the boiling jam; it defeats the purpose, which is to cool the hot jam to room temperature.) This cool-down will take a couple of minutes. Touch your finger to the bottom of the tablespoon. Is it still warm? If it has cooled completely, hold the tablespoon with the handle upright and the spoon end pointing downward.

Examine the jam as it rolls off the spoon. Is it a singular blob or does it spread apart into separate streams? You are looking for one steady ooze as it slides off the spoon. It should not be watery, and it should not separate. If it does separate, cook for another few minutes and do the spoon test again, with a new frozen spoon. Hint: Always freeze four spoons. You may not use them all, but it's better to have them than to want them.

large wooden spoon until well mixed. Cook for 5 minutes, then remove the pot from the heat.

Let the cherries sit at room temperature for at least 4 hours, tossing occasionally, so the juice will be drawn from the fruit, dissolving the sugar.

Set the stockpot over high heat, bring the jam to a full rolling boil, and cook for another 5 minutes, stirring constantly so the sugar won't burn.

Reduce the heat to medium, and allow the jam to cook, stirring frequently as it reduces and thickens. Once thickened, remove it from the heat, stir in the bourbon, and allow it to cool to room temperature.

Once cooled, check the set of the preserves using the spoon test. If the jam is too loosely set, simmer for another 5 to 10 minutes; then remove the mixture from the heat and repeat the test. Continue simmering and stirring, occasionally repeating the test, until the jam is the right consistency.

Once cooled, ladle the jam into clean jars. Store in the refrigerator for up to 1 month.

❧ Bourbon: Nature's Preservative

We all know that alcohol is an excellent preservative, so when you're faced with an embarrassment of riches in the form of late June's precious (and briefly offered!) sour cherries, why not combine the two?

If you choose to pit your cherries, I suggest making the job easier by firmly pressing a drinking straw against the dent from where you've pulled the stem, until the pressure of the forward motion is stopped by the pit. Once you've carved a circle, you can gently push out the stone, leaving the fruit intact. Or, you can leave your cherries as nature intended, pits and all.

Bourbon-Preserved Cherries

More a technique than a recipe, preserving cherries in bourbon is embarrassingly simple, and having them on hand to flavor cocktails, spoon over ice cream, or give to friends makes the minimal effort pay off in spades.

- Wash a jar and its lid in hot, soapy water. There's no need to sterilize it because the sugar, alcohol, and refrigeration will preserve the mixture.
- Layer cherries in the bottom and sprinkle generously with sugar (the tarter the cherries, the heavier hand you'll want with the sugar).
- Repeat until the jar is full to within a half inch of the top.
- Slowly pour top-shelf bourbon over the cherries, permeating the cracks and allowing it to pool in the bottom of the jar.
- Keep the jar in the refrigerator, and let it age for about a month before sampling. From time to time, tip the jar over, and shake it, encouraging the cherries to marinate and the bourbon and sugar to develop into a rich syrup.
- When made with this recipe, sour cherries are potent and flavorful, especially when served with a selection of creamy cheeses, or alongside a selection of strongly spiced summer sausages, jerky, or other preserved meats.

Do Cherry Pits Really Contain Cyanide?

In a word, yes. Or rather, a cyanide and sugar compound called amygdalin, which degrades into cyanide when metabolized. Still, many chefs and home cooks feel comfortable with the risk, based on the small amounts and methods of preparation that they use. Cherry pits contain cyanide, as do the kernels of many other fruits, including apples and apricots. Is there enough to harm the average home cook and normal fruit consumers? Unlikely. Without being chewed or mechanically broken up, the amount of harmful chemicals released from fruit pits is likely to be trace. Many recipe books advocate the cooking of certain fruits with their pits because this method extracts a particular bitter almond flavor from the inner kernel, or noyaux. I feel comfortable cooking the fruit with pits, and the unique flavor really appeals to me. Traditional recipes for the custard-like dessert clafouti call for unpitted cherries in order to capture this subtle flavoring. The choice is yours. Some people prefer to be safe than sorry.

Bourbon Baked-Apple Butter

Eating apple butter is like tasting the soul of an apple. Reduced to what's essential, a mere teaspoon recounts the flavor of an orchard. Silky smooth, deep, and earthy, people often think it's packed with dairy butter. I use just the smallest dab of butter to grease my baking dish, but apart from that, apple butter is low in fat and bursting with healthful fruit. That's not why I eat it, though. I love the texture and the flavor. The addition of spices and bourbon turn it into something almost like a pudding. Slather it on creamy cheeses, spoon it onto custard, stir it into pudding, or use it as a topping on ice cream. Or simply pile it onto buttered French bread to make what's basically a deconstructed pastry.

Makes about 1½ cups

2 tablespoons butter
3 pounds Jonagold, Braeburn, or Cortland apples, peeled, cored, and cut into quarters
3 cups apple cider
2 tablespoons butter, for greasing pan
2 tablespoons lemon juice
¼ cup bourbon
¼ teaspoon ground cinnamon
½ teaspoon ground cloves

In a Dutch oven set over medium-high heat, combine the butter and apples. Cook until the apples soften slightly, about 5 to 7 minutes.

Add the cider and bring the mixture to a boil. Once large bubbles are popping on the surface, reduce the heat and simmer on low, partially covered and stirring occasionally, until very soft, about 40 minutes.

Preheat oven to 250 degrees F. Butter a 9 x 13-inch glass baking dish.

Using a potato masher, mash the softened apples to a pulp. Remove the Dutch oven from heat and add the lemon juice, bourbon, cinnamon, and cloves. Using an immersion blender, puree the mixture until smooth.

Pour apple mixture evenly into the baking dish. Transfer to the oven and bake, stirring occasionally, until thickened and reduced, about 3 to 4 hours.

Once the mixture has thickened, remove the baking dish from the oven, set on a wire rack, and let the apple butter cool before serving.

Store in the refrigerator, in a tightly lidded container, for up to 1 week.

❧ *Bourbon Fact*

The proof's in the pudding . . . um, bourbon.

"Proof" describes alcoholic strength. One point of proof equals 0.5 percent alcohol. (Thus, 100 proof equals 50 percent alcohol.) Long ago, proof was determined by mixing equal amounts of spirits and gunpowder together and lighting it on fire. If the gunpowder didn't ignite, the spirit was too weak. If it flashed, it was too strong. An even burn with a blue flame was said to be "100 percent proved right," setting the standard by which strength was measured.

Bourbon Lemon Curd

⟩ Lemon curd is so bright and cheerful, and the wake-me-up tang makes it a natural spread for breakfast. The tartness of the lemon balances out the sweetness of the sugar. It's like scooping the middle out of a lemon meringue pie.

A workhorse of an ingredient, you can use lemon curd as a garnish for cheesecake, a filling for cookies, or as a layer in a trifle. A word of advice: use the best butter you can find for that quality of dairy-rich creaminess.

Beginning cooks might have heard warnings about curdling and the need to strain out flecks of cooked egg white. (Whites cook faster than yolks.) It's true that with some curd-making techniques, the cook has to vigilantly stir the pot at all times in order to ensure a silken texture.

With this recipe you can relax, because the eggs are blended up front before the mixture is heated. It's as easy to make as a simple batter and always turns out lusciously smooth and lump-free.

Makes about 2 cups

½ cup (1 stick) tablespoons butter
1¼ cups granulated sugar
2 large eggs
3 large egg yolks
⅔ cup lemon juice
Zest of 1 small lemon
1½ tablespoons bourbon
¼ teaspoon salt

In a large mixing bowl, with an electric mixer set on medium-high speed, beat the butter and sugar together until light and fluffy, about 3 minutes.

In a separate bowl, whisk together the whole eggs and egg yolks until fully blended. Then, a little at a time, add the beaten eggs to the creamed butter mixture until smooth, beating after each addition, about 1 minute. Once smooth, mix in the lemon juice, and beat for 1 minute more. (At this point, you'll think the mixture has curdled, but what you're seeing are particles of butter. As the mixture cooks, it will turn velvety.)

Pour the mixture into a medium-sized, heavy-bottomed saucepan and cook over medium heat for 10 to 15 minutes, stirring constantly, until the curd thickens.

Test for set by coating the back of a wooden spoon and running your finger through it. If a distinct track remains, it's done.

Remove the saucepan from the heat and stir in the lemon zest, bourbon, and salt. Cool to room temperature before serving.

Store in the refrigerator, in a tightly lidded container, for up to 3 weeks

Kentucky Plus

> Make a sweeter curd by substituting fresh orange juice and zest for the lemon.

> Fill a graham cracker crust with the curd and top with sliced strawberries for an eye-poppingly gorgeous hot weather treat.

> Spread lemon curd on top of a wheel of brie, and serve it with slices of date-nut bread.

Sweet Golden Chutney with Bourbon

⟩ Used as a condiment, chutney is generally preserved using vinegar (think piccalilli or chow chow). This dessert version relies on bourbon in place of vinegar. This is a small-batch recipe, and rather than sterilize all of my canning equipment, I store it in the refrigerator. This fruity delicacy can be used in a number of delicious ways, but I've been known to simply eat it by the dishful with butter cookies on the side, or ladle a scoop over a mound of cottage cheese for a somewhat angelic snack that satisfies my sweet tooth.

Kentucky Plus

⟩ Scoop the flesh out of a pineapple half, fill it halfway with mascarpone cheese, and top with chutney. Flank with digestive biscuits and water crackers.

⟩ Warm the chutney, and serve over a mix of coconut ice cream and raspberry sorbet.

⟩ Use the chutney as the jam layer in a winter trifle.

Makes about 5 cups

¾ cup light brown sugar, packed
3 cups fresh pineapple, finely diced
2 Granny Smith apples, peeled, cored, and diced
2 firm pears, peeled, cored, and diced
1 cup golden raisins
½ tablespoon allspice
¼ cup fresh ginger, peeled and finely chopped
½ teaspoon salt
¾ cup bourbon

In a very large mixing bowl combine the brown sugar, pineapple, apples, pears, raisins, allspice, ginger, and salt. Toss lightly, and let the mixture rest on the countertop covered with a clean dish towel for about an hour, so the flavors can mingle.

Transfer the mixture to a large, heavy-bottomed saucepan set over medium-high heat. Add the bourbon.

Simmer, stirring frequently, for 20 to 30 minutes, until the liquid has reduced and a light syrup has formed.

Cool before serving.

Store in the refrigerator, in a tightly lidded container, for up to 1 week.

Bourbon-Sweetened Stewed Fruit for Ice Creams and Custards

⟩ If you ask me, stewed fruit has gotten a bad rap. I think for some, it calls to mind sad dishes of mushy, unadorned prunes in hospital cafeterias. But the truth is, stewed fruit is a dish made with nature's most appealing jewels, heated up to soften the texture and release the buried sweetness. Add bourbon, and top it with ice cream or custard, and you'll create the perfect dessert to relax and reward yourself and your guests.

Makes about 2 cups

1 cup chopped red rhubarb
1 cup quartered strawberries
1 cup peeled and chopped fresh apricots
 Fresh ginger, a piece about as big as your thumb, peeled and diced
3 teaspoons granulated sugar, plus more to taste
¼ cup bourbon
1 tablespoon lemon juice

In a large, heavy-bottomed saucepan set over medium heat, combine all ingredients.

Cover and simmer gently, stirring occasionally, until the fruit has softened, about 15 minutes.

Remove the lid, raise the heat to medium-high, and continue to cook, stirring frequently. Once the liquid has reduced and a light syrup has formed, remove the pan from heat. Serve warm.

Store in the refrigerator, in a tightly lidded container, for up to 1 week.

Traditional Orange Marmalade with Bourbon

You know what's great about marmalade? The bitterness. You either like it or you don't. Sure, it's lightened up with sugar to offer some sweet balance, but the bitterness is the thing. Some marmalades remove pith, but for die-hard fans, that robs the spread of its distinction. There's no need to add pectin, since it's abundant in the pith and peel. And while there's also no need to add bourbon, I sure like to.

Makes about 4 pints

6 large thin-skinned oranges, washed
6 cups water
1 cup bourbon
1 tablespoon lemon juice
8 cups sugar
Pinch salt
Pinch ground cloves

Put four tablespoons in the freezer to chill. You'll use at least one of these to perform the "spoon test" for doneness (page 169).

Using a mandoline, cut the oranges into the thinnest slices possible (try for ⅛ inch), removing and discarding the seeds as you work. Then, stack the slices and use a chef's knife to quarter them.

In an 8-quart stainless steel pot set over high heat, combine the oranges, water, bourbon, lemon juice, sugar, salt, and cloves, and bring to a boil. Once boiling, reduce the heat and simmer, stirring frequently, for 30 to 40 minutes or until the fruit is very soft.

Perform the spoon test (page 169). If the mixture is thin and runs easily, it is not ready. If so, return the pot to the heat and simmer another 5 to 10 minutes and perform the test again, repeating until the marmalade is set.

Once done, remove the pot from the heat, and allow the marmalade to cool to room temperature. Ladle it into clean jars, and seal.

Store in the refrigerator, in tightly lidded jars, for up to 1 month.

Apricot and Bourbon Butter

Unlike the recipe for Bourbon Baked-Apple Butter (page 172), this fruit butter recipe contains real butter, and plenty of it. It's so simple to make, even the most inexperienced home cook can nail it on the first try. Its fruity-sweet flavor and satisfying, creamy heft will call you back to the kitchen again and again. And don't forget the bourbon. Oh, the bourbon! We go through this like, well, a knife through butter. I like to make big batches, and freeze it. In a tightly sealed container, it keeps well in the freezer for two weeks.

Bourbon Fact

It may look frilly, but it packs a wallop!

The mint julep has been associated with the Kentucky Derby and promoted by Churchill Downs since 1938. Each year almost 120,000 juleps are sold during the two-day period that includes the running of the Kentucky Oaks and the Kentucky Derby.

Makes about 2½ cups

1 cup dried apricots, chopped
½ cup bourbon
⅓ cup light brown sugar, packed
2 cups (4 sticks) butter, at room temperature
½ teaspoon salt

In a medium-sized, heavy-bottomed saucepan, off the heat, combine the apricots and bourbon and let the mixture rest for 15 minutes.

Turn the heat to high, and bring the mixture to a boil, stirring constantly, about 10 minutes. Once the mixture is boiling, carefully set the top on fire with a long match.

When the flames begin to die down, add the brown sugar, reduce the heat to medium, and simmer until the sugar is dissolved, stirring frequently.

Transfer the mixture to the bowl of a food processor and let it cool.

Add the butter and salt, and process until smooth, about 3 minutes.

Serve immediately, or store in a tightly lidded container in the refrigerator for up to 1 week.

9 Dessert Drinks

When I was a child, mom and pop dairies were still a staple of community life. We had an insulated box by our back door into which a milkman delivered milk. I'm not quite old enough to remember men in white uniforms leaving glass milk bottles with a paper seal. My neighborhood was served by a milk truck that operated the "modern" way. My kids beg me to tell them about what they see as a very old-fashioned concept they've read about in quaint storybooks. It's hard to paint them a picture of the late 1960s-style "space-age" plastic bags of milk that we'd rest in the dedicated bright orange holders, and snip the corners off of to enable pouring.

Our dairy was Ehrler's, and my heart broke just a little when they went out of business not many years ago. Not only did my family agree that their ice cream was the freshest in town, but I was also told that my grandfather, an electrician by trade, hung the orange-and-white sign at the flagship store. Every kid in town knew this sign. It featured a cow standing next to a windmill that turned evenly and constantly, quite a sight in the days before advertising went digital, with ubiquitous flat screens at every turn.

It's not a stretch to imagine adding bourbon to sweet, frozen drinks. You may have thought of doing it yourself, once or twice. Here are some recipes to help you make it happen.

Bourbon Pumpkin-Pie Milkshake

A favorite autumn treat around my house is a slice of warm pumpkin pie topped with a scoop of vanilla ice cream. For an added kick of comfort, my husband and I take ours with a smooth glass of bourbon, straight up, thank you very much.

In our house, we have no problem with offering the kids sweets made with bourbon as a flavoring. However, I like this milkshake concoction made like a cocktail. When I make these shakes for the whole family, I do two batches: a "virgin" batch for the kids, and a loaded batch for the parents.

Makes 4 milkshakes

2 cups vanilla ice cream
½ cup whole milk
½ cup half-and-half
¼ cup bourbon
¾ cup canned packed pumpkin
   (not pumpkin pie filling)
1 tablespoon pumpkin pie spice
½ teaspoon cinnamon
½ teaspoon salt
½ cup Bourbon and Sorghum Buttercream
   (page 140), for garnish
½ cup crushed gingersnaps (from about 4
   cookies), for garnish

In the bowl of a blender, combine the ice cream, milk, half-and-half, bourbon, pumpkin, pumpkin pie spice, cinnamon, and salt. Blend on medium-high until smooth.

Rim 4 tall glasses with a light coat of frosting, about ½ inch down the outside walls, and roll the glasses in the gingersnap crumbs. Divide the mixture among the glasses, and serve.

Spiked Egg-White Cocoa

⟩ Growing up in Louisville, I often had the thrill of waking to feet of snow where there had been none the night before. The side-porch steps to my grandmother's Germantown shotgun house were probably only about as tall as an adult's waist, but when I was a kid, jumping off of those steps into the snow was like jumping into a deep swimming pool. My grandfather would bundle up (always wearing his felt fedora circa 1958) and patiently accompany me out to "shovel the walk." Not much progress was made shoveling, but I had fun diving and playing until my ears went numb. My grandmother gave us hot chocolate to warm us while our clothes dried out over the heating registers. I suspect my grandfather's mug had a shot of bourbon for extra heat.

Makes about 4 mugs

4 ounces dark chocolate (70% cacao), roughly
  chopped
2 cups whole milk
1 cup half-and-half
½ teaspoon ground cinnamon
1 tablespoon light brown sugar, packed
2 tablespoons unsweetened cocoa powder (I like
  Scharffen Berger's)
Pinch salt
2 large egg whites, cold
½ cup bourbon

In a medium-sized, heavy-bottomed saucepan set over low heat, combine the chocolate, milk, half-and-half, cinnamon, brown sugar, cocoa powder, and salt, stirring gently and constantly to help the chocolate and sugar dissolve.

In a separate small bowl, whisk the egg whites until soft peaks form.

Increase the heat under the milk mixture to medium-high, and whisk constantly to froth, keeping the temperature to just below boiling.

When the mixture in the pan has reduced a little and is frothy, about 5 minutes, remove it from the heat, and briskly whisk in the beaten egg whites.

Add the bourbon, and stir gently to combine.

Divide the hot cocoa among 4 mugs, and serve.

Store in the refrigerator, in a tightly lidded jar or bottle, for up to 1 week. Mix well, and heat before serving.

❧ *What's an Egg Cream, and How Do You Make One?*

If you go by the original recipe, an egg cream is little more than milk, chocolate syrup, and seltzer. That description may sound humdrum, but it's the combination of simple ingredients built with the perfect technique that elevates this soda-fountain delight. Here's why it's good: milk is creamy and comforting, you can customize the syrup to personalize the flavor profile, and everything's better with bubbles.

1. Use whole milk for texture and body. Don't cheat yourself by using the watery, low-fat stuff. Enjoy this rare treat to the fullest.

2. When you think it's cold enough, make it colder—refrigerate or freeze tools and ingredients: syrup, milk, seltzer, spoon, and glass.

3. Layer the milk in first. Start with a depth of around two inches.

4. Painfully slowly, add the seltzer. Do it in super slo-mo. Drizzle it in until the foam just hits at reaching the top of the glass. Careful! One extra smidge and it'll run over.

5. Add the syrup and, using a long spoon, quickly but lightly stir from the bottom of the cup, using the motion you'd use to beat an egg.

Bourbon and Honey Egg Cream

⟩ This drink comforts in summer or winter. It lulls your taste buds with the cool creaminess of milk, the earthy, comforting sweetness of honey, and the woody brace of bourbon. If you've had a hard day, this is the pre-bedtime drink to soothe and relax your nerves.

Makes 1 drink

½ cup whole milk
2 tablespoons honey
2 tablespoons bourbon
Seltzer

Pour the milk into a very cold, tall glass.

Drizzle in the honey, and stir briskly with a long spoon.

Add the bourbon, and stir briskly again.

Slowly pour seltzer down the side of the glass until nearly at the top. Stir well and serve.

Kentucky Plus

⟩ Add 1 tablespoon Toasted Almond and Bourbon Syrup (page 139), and substitute 1 tablespoon store-bought chocolate syrup for the honey to make a Bourbon Ball Egg Cream.

⟩ For a bright, fresh, breakfast pick-me-up, wash and hull 4 large, ripe strawberries and mash them, along with 1 teaspoon granulated sugar, using a potato masher. Stir in with the honey.

Classic Kentucky Eggnog

I put eggnog in the same category as a mint julep: an iron fist in a velvet glove. Deceptively genteel and fine-mannered, these drinks are dressed-up ways to usher large jiggers of bourbon past the lips. Nothing wrong with that. I say bring it on!

I like this recipe because it's light and airy. The addition of beaten egg whites is the key. (See "Raw Eggs—Safe or Not?" on page 94.) Stir in fluffy whipped cream, and this drinks like a dessert. Don't forget the bourbon, though . . . Sweet and rich, I've been known to have two or three of these before the bourbon sneaks up and reminds me of its presence.

Makes about 1 quart

5 eggs, cold and separated
¾ cup granulated sugar, divided
2 cups whole milk
1½ cups bourbon
½ teaspoon salt
2 teaspoons pure vanilla extract
1 teaspoon freshly grated nutmeg,
   plus more for garnish
1 cup heavy cream, divided

In a medium-sized mixing bowl, whisk the egg yolks together with ½ cup sugar until creamy and the sugar begins to dissolve. Stir in the milk, bourbon, salt, vanilla, and ½ teaspoon of nutmeg. Set aside.

In a large mixing bowl, whisk the egg whites until soft peaks form, about 3 minutes. Add the remaining sugar, and whisk until stiff peaks form, about 5 minutes.

In another medium-sized mixing bowl, beat ½ cup heavy cream until light and fluffy, about 5 minutes.

Fold the egg whites into the whipped cream.

Pour the yolk mixture into a punch bowl, and gently spoon on the egg white and whipped cream mixture. Dust the top with grated nutmeg, and chill for an hour before serving.

Store any leftovers in the refrigerator, in a tightly lidded jar or bottle, for up to 3 days.

Cooked and Spiked Eggnog Custard

For those who prefer not to cook with raw eggs, this drinkable custard is a great way to get your holiday season on.

Festive, rich, and potent, this custard is the version my family made back in the day because everyone loved the thick richness and the way that it left a lickable coating on the lips.

Makes about 1 quart

5 egg yolks
¾ cup granulated sugar
2 cups whole milk, divided
1 cup heavy cream, divided
½ teaspoon salt
2 teaspoons pure vanilla extract
1 teaspoon freshly grated nutmeg, plus more for garnish
1½ cups bourbon

In a medium-sized metal mixing bowl, whisk together the egg yolks and sugar until creamy and the sugar begins to dissolve.

Stir in 1 cup of the milk, ½ cup of the cream, the salt, the vanilla, and ½ teaspoon of the nutmeg. Set the metal bowl over a pot of simmering water and whisk constantly for 5 minutes.

Remove the metal bowl from the pot, and refrigerate the yolk mixture until well chilled.

When ready to serve, stir in the remaining 1 cup milk and ½ cup cream; then stir in the bourbon.

Dust the top with grated nutmeg, and serve.

Store in the refrigerator, in a tightly lidded jar or bottle, for up to three days.

Bourbon Fact

Life is short. Have dessert, and a shot of bourbon, first.

There are about 70 calories in one fluid ounce of bourbon, and about 105 in a "jigger," or shot glass, which commonly holds an ounce and a half.

High-Octane Coffee-and-Eggnog Frappe

⟫ You can pretend this is a coffee drink, but who's kidding whom? Like popular frappucinos and mocha lattes, it's just a clever way to deny that you're having dessert in a glass. But why deny it? I embrace it whole hog! Sipping one of these while I prepare the New Year's Day supper gives me the sustenance I need, and just the celebratory punch I'm looking for to kick off a festive home holiday.

Makes 6 servings

1 cup Classic Kentucky Eggnog (page 185) or
    Cooked and Spiked Eggnog Custard (page
    186), or store-bought eggnog
1 pint vanilla ice cream
½ cup whole milk
1 cup bourbon
¼ cup espresso or strongly brewed dark coffee,
    cold
Bourbon Whipped Cream (page 71), for garnish
Finely ground espresso or instant coffee crystals,
    for garnish

In the bowl of a blender, combine the eggnog, ice cream, milk, bourbon, and espresso, and blend on high until smooth.

Divide among 6 tall glasses, top with Bourbon Whipped Cream, and dust with espresso or coffee crystals.

Store in the freezer, in a lidded jar or bottle. Bring to room temperature and stir before serving.

A Shot and a Beer Punch Slush

I'm not going to lie to you: I love the kitschy fussiness of a punch bowl. Have one with the little hooks to hang the glasses on the side? I'm in heaven.

One of my favorite things about old-school punches is the quiet deception. "Oh, punch!" one might think. "No harm in having a glass or two to refresh during this garden party" (or wedding reception, or graduation celebration, or what have you). And there is no harm, really. But one should always be prepared for the "spike." Unless served at a toddler's birthday alongside a clown cake, there's probably a punch to that punch. This recipe goes down smooth . . . real smooth. The slushy citrus pop will quench your thirst and cool you down. Just make sure you're near a lawn chair if you have more than one.

Makes one standard punchbowl (serves 18 to 20)

5 cups water
2 cups brewed tea, cold
2 cups bourbon
1 (12-ounce) can beer (use pilsner or lager)
1 cup granulated sugar
1 (6-ounce) can frozen orange juice concentrate, thawed

1 (7.5 ounce) package frozen lemon juice concentrate, thawed (not lemonade)
Lemon wheels, for garnish
Orange wheels, for garnish

In a large mixing bowl, combine the water, tea, bourbon, beer, sugar, orange juice concentrate, and lemon concentrate, and mix until the sugar is completely dissolved.

Pour into 3 heavy-duty, gallon-size freezer bags. (Do not overfill.) Make sure the bags are tightly sealed, and lay them in a deep roasting pan or 3 separate bowls in order to catch leaks.

Freeze until 1 hour before serving.

To serve, transfer the frozen mixture into a punch bowl and let it thaw, muddling it with a wooden spoon every 10 minutes. As the punch melts, add ice. Float lemon and orange wheels on the surface to garnish.

Store in the freezer, in heavy-duty, gallon-size freezer bags set in bowls, for up to 1 month.

Strawberry Bourbon Milkshake with White Chocolate Mint Mousse

Nothing says springtime in Kentucky like strawberries and bourbon. I remember when I was a little kid, venturing out on late June days to the U-pick-it farm. Excited by the grown-up assignment, and armed with my own basket, I'd haul in a good yield for about half an hour. After that, I spent most of my time chasing bugs in the dirt, and quenching my thirst by eating summer-ripe strawberries bursting with juice warm from the sun. When I was a kid, the men merely went along for the ride, and it wasn't long before they left the women to do the work, while they drank cans of Falls City beer from coolers in their cars, and took long draws from pocket flasks of bourbon.

Those flavors reign in this milkshake. I like to complement them with an unexpected mousse. The white chocolate is intensely rich, even softened with the airy egg white (see the raw egg discussion on page 94), so a little dab will do you. I cut it with just a hint of sharp mint flavor.

Makes 4 milkshakes

FOR THE MOUSSE
8 ounces white chocolate, chopped (I like Ghirardelli)
¾ cup heavy cream
1 large egg white, cold
2 drops peppermint extract

FOR THE MILKSHAKES
1 cup strawberries, quartered
¼ cup bourbon
4 cups vanilla ice cream
1 teaspoon vanilla
¼ teaspoon salt
4 whole strawberries, for garnish
4 sprigs mint, for garnish

TO MAKE THE MOUSSE
Put the white chocolate in a small metal bowl, and set this bowl over a medium-sized saucepan over simmering water until the chocolate melts, stirring occasionally with a heat-proof, silicone spatula. Once the chocolate is melted, remove the bowl from the pan, and set it aside.

In a separate medium-sized mixing bowl, combine the cream, egg white, and peppermint extract. Using an electric mixer, beat until soft peaks form, about 3 minutes.

Add the whipped cream to the cooled white chocolate, and gently fold together using a rubber spatula.

Refrigerate for at least 15 minutes, to chill and set.

TO MAKE THE MILKSHAKES

In the bowl of a blender, combine the strawberries and bourbon, and puree until smooth, about 3 minutes.

Add the ice cream, vanilla, and salt, and blend again, about 3 minutes.

TO ASSEMBLE

Pour the milkshake into 4 tall glasses, and top with the mousse. Serve with a long spoon and a straw. Garnish the glass with a whole strawberry, slit ¾ of the way up from the bottom, and a sprig of mint.

Store the milkshake in the freezer, in a tightly lidded container, for up to 2 weeks, and thaw slightly before serving. Store the mousse in the refrigerator in a tightly lidded container for up to 3 days.

❧ *How To Make an Old-School Egg Shake*

The top two things you want out of an egg shake are froth and flavor. Try my tips for concocting the best of the best, every time.

1. Crack a whole egg into a cocktail shaker and shake with gusto for 5 to 10 seconds. (Make sure your egg is as cold as possible, without freezing.)

2. Add 2 or 3 ice cubes, plus the cream, and shake vigorously for another 5 to 10 seconds.

3. Add your flavorings, and shake briskly for another 10 seconds.

4. Remove the small half of the shaker, and add the seltzer to the shaken mixture until the foam is about two-thirds of the way up the big half. Pour the liquid back and forth from small to big, in order to blend and aerate.

5. From a height of about six inches, slowly pour the egg shake mixture into a chilled serving glass.

Bourbon and Ginger Egg Shake

When someone mentions soda fountains, images of wholesome, family eateries spring to mind. In their early days, however, when the ice cream counters shared real estate with actual chemists' labs in the corners of drugstores, soda fountains were meeting places for men; and cocaine, caffeine, alcohol, and other "medicinals" were dispensed freely. The egg shake enjoyed popularity as a sweet treat, and as a restorative and a health-booster, as the raw egg in the recipe was thought to boost vitality. Even today—especially in cold weather—people gravitate toward creamy, rich egg drinks like egg creams, eggnogs, and egg shakes as soothing, comforting fare. Add the warmth of bourbon, and you have a snack, a dessert, and a cocktail all rolled into one!

Makes 1 drink

1 whole egg
2 tablespoons heavy cream
3 tablespoons bourbon
1 teaspoon fresh ginger, peeled and finely chopped
1 tablespoon honey
Seltzer

In a cocktail shaker, shake the egg until it's frothy. Put 2 or 3 ice cubes in the shaker, add the cream, and shake for about 15 seconds. Add the bourbon, ginger, and honey, and shake one final time. Pour in the seltzer until the foam comes to the top of the shaker, then pour the mixture back and forth from shaker half to shaker half a couple of times until well combined. Pour into a tall, chilled glass and serve.

Warm Chocolate and Bourbon Silk

❧ Doesn't the word silk make you think of the Kentucky Derby? From the brightly colored racing silks worn by the jockeys, to the silk cocktail dresses that the ladies pair with their breathtaking hats, to the fluid movement of a thoroughbred's gallop, to the silver-tongued compliments paid by the gentlemen in their seersucker suits, it just fits.

This drink is all that smooth excellence boiled down into one cup. Enjoy it early, walking through spring mist and dewy grass as you greet the waking horses.

Makes 6 mugs

½ cup semisweet chocolate chips
¼ cup white corn syrup
¼ cup water
½ teaspoon pure vanilla extract
1 cup heavy cream
4 cups milk
6 ounces bourbon
Cocoa powder, for dusting

In a medium-sized, heavy-bottomed saucepan set over low heat, combine the chocolate chips, corn syrup, water, and vanilla. Warm the mixture, stirring often, until the chocolate has melted. Remove from heat and chill in the refrigerator for at least 15 minutes.

Pour the cream into a medium-sized mixing bowl, and beat, using an electric mixer set to medium-high, until soft peaks form.

Gradually add the chocolate mixture, and beat on medium-low until it mounds. Chill in the refrigerator for at least 30 minutes.

To serve, heat the milk in a medium-sized saucepan set over medium heat. If bubbles start to form at the edges, reduce the heat. You want the milk steaming hot, but not boiling.

Divide the warm milk evenly among 6 mugs.

Stir 4 tablespoons of the chocolate mixture into each mug, and stir to combine.

Add 1 ounce of bourbon to each mug, and stir one turn. Serve immediately.

Store in the refrigerator, in a tightly lidded jar or bottle, for up to 1 week. Shake to combine, and heat before serving.

Mint Julep Granitas with Citrus-Cream Topping

⟩ Nothing says spring garden party like the refreshing bite of a cold and tangy granita, and with the flavors of the Kentucky Derby, this simple and elegant dessert will take your race-day lunch to the next level. Just like its cocktail namesake, this dessert drink is a wolf in sheep's clothing—its appearance is gracious and civilized, but it quietly wields unexpected strength and power. Just like any good southerner.

Makes 8 drinks

FOR THE GRANITAS
Juice of 1 small lime
2½ cups water
1½ cups sugar
⅔ cup fresh mint leaves, finely minced
1½ cups, plus 12 ounces bourbon

FOR THE CITRUS CREAM TOPPING
¾ cup heavy cream
½ teaspoon sugar
1 teaspoon lemon juice
Zest of half a lemon
8 lime wedges, for garnish
Mint sprigs, for garnish

TO MAKE THE GRANITAS
Using the heel of your hand, firmly roll the lime on the countertop. Cut it in half across the meridian, and squeeze out the juice into a small bowl, using your hand. Use the tines of a fork to break the cells and release more juice, taking care not to scrape in any pith.

In a medium saucepan set over medium-high heat, combine the water and sugar and bring the mixture to a boil to create a simple syrup. Stir in the mint. Remove the pan from the heat, and let it cool completely.

Strain the liquid through a fine-meshed wire sieve or cheesecloth into an 8 x 8-inch square baking dish, and discard the mint. Stir in 1½ cups bourbon and the lime juice.

Freeze for 1 hour, then scrape the slush with a fork to break up the ice crystals. Return the pan to the freezer for another hour or two, or until it freezes almost solid. (If freezing overnight or for a long period, plan to let the mixture thaw on the countertop to a slushy, half-frozen consistency for 30 minutes before scraping and serving.)

TO MAKE THE CITRUS CREAM

In a medium-sized mixing bowl, combine the cream, sugar, lemon juice, and zest. Using an electric mixer set to medium-high, beat until soft peaks form.

TO ASSEMBLE

Remove the granita mixture from the freezer, and scrape it again with a fork. Scoop the mixture into 8 tall glasses.

Pour 1½ shots of bourbon into each glass, then top with a dollop of citrus cream. Garnish each glass with a lime wedge and a sprig of mint, and serve with a straw and a long spoon.

Store the granita in the freezer, in a tightly lidded container, up to 1 month, thawing and scraping before serving. Store the citrus cream in the refrigerator, in a tightly lidded container, up to 3 days.

❧ *Bourbon Fact*

Honey, can you pick up a gallon of milk and a barrel of bourbon?

A standard bourbon barrel holds 53 gallons of the spirit.

Acknowledgments

Thank you to my Kentucky family. You were there from the start.

The entire team at the University Press of Kentucky has been brilliant. I'm grateful to my editor, Ashley Runyon, for her steadiness and patience. Your sound advice made my book better. Special thanks to David Cobb, Blair Thomas, and Donna Bouvier for your direct support.

Warmest thanks to my excellent photographer, David Bowers. Working with you was a pleasure. I'm lucky to have had a real artist shoot this book.

Deep thanks to my agent, Sharon Bowers. I admire her canny way of visualizing projects and coaxing into place the elements that make them work. Her contributions far exceed those of her on-paper job description.

Thanks, too, to the partners of Miller Bowers Griffin Literary Agency for lending an ear and offering excellent advice born of years of experience representing cookbooks.

And finally, I'd like to thank my New York family for always being on my side. Sam, Rose, and Wolf, you are the reasons I try each day to succeed.

Index